BE YOUR BEST
ENTREPRENEUR
. . . AND BEYOND

Alex McMillan

Q·LEARNING

For UK orders: please contact Bookpoint Ltd, 130 Milton Park, Abingdon, Oxon OX14 4SB.
Telephone: +44 (0) 1235 827720. Fax: +44 (0) 1235 400454. Lines are open 09.00–18.00, Monday to Saturday, with a 24-hour message answering service. You can also order through our website: www.madaboutbooks.com

British Library Cataloguing in Publication Data A catalogue record for this title is available from The British Library.

Library of Congress Catalog Card Number: On file.

This edition, first published in UK 2003 by Hodder Headline Plc, 338 Euston Road, London NW1 3BH

Typeset by Servis Filmsetting Ltd, Manchester, England
Printed in Great Britain for Hodder & Stoughton Educational, a Division of Hodder Headline Plc, 338 Euston Road, London NW1 3BH by Cox & Wyman Ltd, Reading, Berkshire.

Impression number   10 9 8 7 6 5 4 3 2 1
Year   2007 2006 2005 2004 2003For UK orders: please contact Bookpoint Ltd,

Contents

Series Introduction

Perhaps you have had an idea, or wanted to achieve something, but known that you not only need some skills but also help with taking the risk and doing it for real. Maybe you have thought 'it is easy for him/her but not for me . . .'

This series is written for people who haven't got the time (or money) to attend a long training course or who are not lucky enough to be managed and mentored by a star in the field in which they want to succeed. These books will be 'back pocket' resources that will inspire and give practical tips that you can read up on and use in the next few minutes. They will also help you feel confident in taking skills that you already have into new situations at work, home and the community.

Lesley Gosling
Q. Learning

Introduction: Entrepreneur

You have an idea right now that has the potential to be developed into a commercial business. What do you do next? You want practical tips from those that have achieved – the streetwise. How to find, spot, exploit and develop opportunities for example. There is no greater challenge, excitement and satisfying way to spend life than in turning one's ideas into reality.

There are five types of business entrepreneur, and you may be a mix of more than one!

🔖 *Lifestyle Entrepreneurs'* motive is to work at what is their personal passion and hobby.

🔖 *Profit Entrepreneurs* have their focus on making money, their prime, often only objective.

🔖 *Formula Entrepreneurs* go for an already established small business format that can be bought or set up quite easily, such as a franchise or network marketing agency.

- 🕦 *Empire Entrepreneurs* are people planning on being a very large company, the next Bill Gates or Richard Branson. Their motivation is usually a mix of creativity coupled with commercial practicality, strong independence, power and influence.

- 🕦 *Creative Entrepreneurs* cover anyone who originates a new product, process, service, artistic work or invention.

Alex McMillan's personal mission is to help the entrepreneur that he believes is in all of us to progress and prosper.

He started school in Cyprus during the Eoka uprisings, his father serving with the Royal Air Force. Latterly he has been educated in Oxford and London where he achieved degrees in Business and Management.

His career has been focused on executive recruitment and training. He is currently a consultant, coach, tutor, motivator and author to entrepreneurs. He is and has been an entrepreneur (Lifestyle, Creative and Profit) himself and is currently planning a trip across the USA in search of the formula for the American Dream.

Alex to his friends is considered the eternal optimist with a passionate belief and energy for his next project. He lives with his wife Tracy and three children Alex, Zoe and Naomi in Sussex.

CHAPTER 1

What If Your Entrepreneurial Dream Happened?

Every time something happens, positive or negative, I ask myself, where is the opportunity here?

RICHARD LOWDEN

As long as you are going to think anyway, think big.

DONALD TRUMP

WHAT IS AN ENTREPRENEUR?

People have different understandings of the term entrepreneur. The motives of an entrepreneur are numerous. Some are purely focused on making money. Some are totally focused on developing their innovations, and money is just the mechanism that allows it to happen, or even the side-effect of success. Most are after both. So when is an entrepreneur successful? Does making more money make an entrepreneur more successful? Add your own answers to these questions. Part of being a better entrepreneur is doing your own thinking and making your own decisions.

There are two distinct aspects of an entrepreneur:

1 Someone who, through creativity, innovation, foresight and discovery, can identify commercial opportunities around him or her.

2 Someone practical who sees and exploits opportunities for making money successfully.

You are an entrepreneur and wish to be a better one. You may not have even started in sales terms, but the idea is there, or perhaps the determination or desire. You have the entrepreneurial spirit and that flame of enterprise needs to be nurtured and grown to a glowing furnace of fun and success.

WHO WANTS TO BE AN ENTREPRENEUR?

Back in the 1990s, working in my own recruitment business, I was requested by my staff to produce a list of questions to ask new candidates. One of the questions that we used gave us some interesting and unexpected results:

'If we could get you any job in the world, and put on your CV any necessary qualifications, skills and experience, as if by magic, what job would you want?'

Out of the first 1000 people we asked, 912 of them said that their dream job was to run their own business.

Hence the reason and target for this book. Many people want to be entrepreneurs and the economy wants more entrepreneurs to secure the future, yet most people who want to do it never do. So the answers in this book focus on the question: 'How can you become a better entrepreneur?'

Explore this book and follow its treasure trail of tips that have worked before and can help you to achieve your dreams. You will find answers to questions like:

- How do successful entrepreneurs think about money?
- What helps them to make decisions?
- How do they motivate themselves?
- What strategies do they use to recover from setbacks?
- What is it that they do, and you can do too, that gives them their success?

WHO WILL BENEFIT FROM THIS BOOK?

This book is aimed at those that want to start or have started their own enterprise and wish to create personal wealth from it. It covers finance, venture capital, marketing, personnel and training from a practical perspective of what has been proven to work. You will be taking lessons from some of the most successful entrepreneurs.

- ⟳ You want to start your own business, but don't know how.
- ⟳ You are running a business but don't know how to get it to the next stage.
- ⟳ You have an idea but don't know how to turn it into a business.

Right from the start you should read this book with a clear purpose. What exactly does the word entrepreneur mean to you? Where would your ideal success be in this direction? The following list will help you choose:

- ⟳ Financial freedom (not having to work for a living)
- ⟳ Independence
- ⟳ A creative outlet

Fame

 The chance to make serious wealth

If you truly want to succeed at something in your career, all you have to do is make the decision to achieve it. Make success the only option — otherwise you will always wonder what you could have become and could have achieved.

AUSTIN REYNOLDS

Austin exceeded his £1 million cash in the bank target soon after starting in business. He has since multiplied his net worth several times.

AM: What is your career background?

AR: Whilst at school, I noticed that 70 per cent of the properties around where I lived needed preserving with creosote. It was obvious who was a good prospect. I started by knocking on my neighbour's door and soon had a thriving business. I went back to school after the summer and left with one 'O' Level. I wanted to work in sales and I got a job as a trainee in a shipping office. I was fired after eight weeks. This greatly affected me and I decided that my future would not be working for someone else.

At 19 I was offered a job in sales with Morgan Crucible in Leeds. At 20 I was made sales trainer on the back of my success. At 21 years I was made regional sales manager with six staff. At 23 years I was headhunted by a small signage company.

By 25 I knew enough to work for myself. I set up in business from my back bedroom with a telephone, a fax machine and cash to last two months. I took orders from clients with a need for signs and procured suppliers, making sure everything went smoothly, as a middleman. I had no printed stationery or even a vehicle. I moved around by borrowing my dad's, mum's or girlfriend's car. Everyone who visited me, I gave something to deliver on their way home. I set daily targets on a wall chart, and only focused on profit: sales figures do not interest me. When I could consistently reach a target I would increase it. I always had to achieve what I set for myself, at all costs, knowing that in business you sometimes have to be patient.

My philosophy was, don't borrow: buy what you want, when you can afford it. I always expect and deliver an excellent customer service. Honesty, integrity and trust are the most important ingredients to build quality long-term relationships and reputation. I have never had a cash flow problem to this day. I have never had to concern myself with interest rates or bank managers. My sole objective and focus was to put £1 million cash in the bank as soon as possible. I can sleep soundly at night. For three years it was just me, and in my final year I turned over £780,000 and personally earned £280,000. I bought a large house and expanded from this base.

Sales and profits continued to rise year on year and I had soon over £1 million in the bank without any debts, other assets plus, of course, a valuable company. Material things never interested me and I have no need to impress anyone, so the business has continued to grow from there.

When I look at a supplier I look for excellence in price, product, delivery and paperwork. I monitor their performance constantly. Good personal relationships are key with both customers and suppliers. I always pay them promptly, not waiting for payment from my client.

In my business there is nothing unique, compared to competitors, apart from us as individuals. I own the whole firm and believe in having one boss. I also believe that whereas it is unwise to pay too much, it is worse to pay too little and risk quality and value.

I was wondering what to do with the cash mountains that have been rising. So I have set up Austin Reynolds Special Projects and have made some investments developing substantial properties. There were four such projects in the last three years. I wish I had done this earlier as the early nineties were a very good time to invest in properties. I have also set up a consumer credit collection company.

AM: How do you define success?

AR: To be able to sleep at night.

To know when you have finished, i.e. reached your goals.

AM: What advice would you give somebody starting out?

AR: **1** Don't borrow money.

2 Start small, have a big idea, and break it down into manageable chunks.

3 Flash means crash (don't go out and buy a flashy car after an initial success).

4 Know your ultimate goal and keep going.

5 Agree hours of work and play, and stick to them.

6 Work smart and hard.

AM: How do you spot an opportunity?

AR: Think, then follow it through. If I notice a new construction site whilst driving I will stop, reverse and do something about it.

AM: What would you have done differently if you could go back in time?

AR: Invested my surplus cash in property in the early nineties.

AM: How do you motivate yourself when things don't go to plan?

AR: Self-belief. Nobody is as good as I am.

HOW TO SEE THE WORLD DIFFERENTLY

An entrepreneur sees things that others miss. They can see resources or potential resources that can be used or utilized in a more beneficial way than they are being used now.

I asked 912 corporate executives seeking a new position what benefits they saw in such a position. Their answers were:

1 Security
2 Comfort
3 High status
4 Professional experience
5 Maintain high mortgage on home
6 Good pension
7 Training
8 Interesting work

I then asked them how they saw the self-employed /entrepreneur option:

1 Insecure, home at risk

2 Danger and vulnerability

3 No regular salary

4 Most fail

5 Independence

6 Freedom

7 Unlimited potential income and capital gain

8 Early retirement or not at all if you don't want to

I then asked the same questions to a number of entrepreneurs/ self-employed people.

How do you see a corporate executive position?

1 In prison, told what to do

2 Regular salary and benefits

3 A boss to report to

4 Office politics necessary to succeed and survive

5 Limited potential to grow; not paid what worth

6 Insecure future

7 Not able to express own ideas

8 High risk; all eggs in one basket

How do you see self-employment/entrepreneurship?

1 Security

2 Financial freedom

3 Outlet for creativity

4 Independence

5 Own boss

6 Potentially unlimited income

7 Potentially unlimited capital gain

8 Paid what I am worth

HOW EASILY CAN YOU BECOME A SUCCESSFUL ENTREPRENEUR?

🖎 Everyone can be a successful entrepreneur.

🖎 Every entrepreneur can be a better one.

Everything you can see around you – the company you work for, every company you have ever bought something from – was created by an entrepreneur with a vision.

Being an entrepreneur is no more than a decision. To be a rock star, dancer, architect, actor, advertising executive, coach or pilot takes talent and training, but to be an entrepreneur is merely a decision. That is all you have to do. It is often unnerving at first, but you can be professionally free. The next step is to become financially free. This is the surest way to eliminate all fears. As one of the entrepreneurs interviewed for this book said, 'I am not motivated by cash: I am motivated by having more choices and I figured that you have more choices with cash than without it.'

Progress now

What changes will you have to make in order to become an even better entrepreneur?

_____

_____

_____

_____

_____

_____

WHAT STOPS YOU BEING AN EVEN BETTER ENTREPRENEUR?

- What stops you starting?
- What stops you thinking of an idea?
- What stops you knowing what business to run?
- What stops you getting from a small to a large company?
- What stops you being an even better entrepreneur?

Your particular 'what stops you . . .?' question depends on where your entrepreneurial career is right now. To answer this you need to know what stage you are at. If you are still at the dreamer stage or on the road to getting going, look at the first question.

The focus of the question is interesting in as much as it assumes that you have control, or at least can take control. This is one of the fundamental rules for successful entrepreneurship. You have to control the world around you and not let it control you. Entrepreneurship is far more about guts than it is about brains. You must focus on your goal, rather than on what might happen if it goes wrong.

HOW TO MAKE A MILLION

To be a successful entrepreneur is a lot easier than you may think. Thinking it is hard or that you won't make it can be greater stoppers of success than anything out there in the economy. All your experiences will allow you to increase your progress rate towards your goals. In all situations you must focus on the positive side, not the negative.

Progress now

Which of the following do you think could make you £1 million fastest?

a)   A new tasty meat pie.

b)   A piece of software that will translate 15 major business languages.

c)   A new audio series on practical steps to increase sales.

d)   A real estate opportunity in the sun offering 100 per cent mortgages.

When asked, most entrepreneurs put the answers in the following order: b) c) a) d). Why do you think that was?

ON BEING A HAPPY ENTREPRENEUR

This book will share with you the secrets of success learnt from successful entrepreneurs. However, there is perhaps a price to pay. The success formula involves adapting your values, beliefs and attitudes, which inevitably means changes. Many great entrepreneurs, whilst successful with money, are very unsuccessful with other aspects of their life. So this book includes a chapter on how to make changes and be a better entrepreneur without paying an unacceptable price. In other words, how to have your cake, eat it and still make money from selling it.

Progress now

What decision can you make right now to help you become a millionaire through your own enterprise?

_____

_____

CHAPTER 2

What Type of Entrepreneur Are You Going to Be?

If you hear a voice within you saying, 'You are not a painter,' then by all means paint . . . and that voice will be silenced.

VINCENT VAN GOGH

There is not a person anywhere that is not capable of doing more than he thinks he can.

HENRY FORD

HOW DO YOU GET STARTED?

How you start depends on your motivations. The most common career goal of aspiring entrepreneurs is to be able to control their own destiny. This holds true for each of the five categories of entrepreneur below. Each category can be started on a part-time or sole trader basis (many larger enterprises started this way). Those who wanted to get bigger did so in reaction to their market demand.

Many start by working part time whilst maintaining their main income. This can provide a second vocation that could be expanded should redundancy strike. When practical, this choice can provide a safe bridge towards becoming fully independent. Others go for it, putting in all their personal resources. Others raise venture capital. This chapter looks at what being an entrepreneur means and discusses each of the categories. By the end you will be in a position to consider what type of entrepreneur you want to be.

You can start on your own, even part time, for most types of enterprise, whatever your ultimate goals are. Starting small is the ideal way to test the market and get lots of live feedback without any major commitment. Then you can risk more resources behind your ideas from a situation of growing confidence.

Progress now

If you have not started a business, tick the category below
which applies to you. If you are looking for finance you will
need very convincing answers to this question: 'How can I
practically manage expansion, making sure that I have the
market before increasing costs?'

- [ ] You want to go it alone, i.e. self-employed, usually though not
  necessarily in your current trade or profession: plumber, mechanic,
  builder, accountant, solicitor, journalist, consultant, coach.

- [ ] You want or have your own business yet wish to remain small and
  independent after having achieved financial and vocational
  freedom.

- [ ] You have creative ideas or have access to creative ideas and have a
  long-term vision to build a very substantial enterprise.

- [ ] You want to build your own business as part of a larger group, for
  example through franchising or network marketing.

- [ ] You want to buy a business.

- [ ] You are an inventor, artist or other originator of new things.

WHAT ARE THE KEY QUALITIES OF AN ENTREPRENEUR?

Innovation, **creativity**, **risk taking**, **independence** and a **strong character** are the heart of entrepreneurship. An entrepreneur is a person who has decided to take control of their future and become self-employed, usually but not necessarily by creating their own unique business, product or service. Entrepreneurs thus add value to society by changing what the consumer wants and needs.

Entrepreneurs compete with themselves, always wanting to improve their own performance. They never believe they have reached their potential and know that success or failure lies within their personal control or influence. You will need strength of character to help you through your challenges and maintain your sense of meaningful purpose. It will also encourage people to do business with you. If they don't trust your word and a handshake, your attractive terms are unlikely to be accepted.

WHAT DOES IT TAKE TO BECOME A BETTER ENTREPRENEUR?

What images does the word **entrepreneur** conjure up in your mind? For most people they are attractive ones of adventure, freedom, independence, fast cars, luxury houses, holidays, success and wealth. These are certainly real and the rewards of success. Like everything worth having though, there are some challenges and achievements along the way.

Hard work is a common habit of successful entrepreneurs. Yet, to be effective, hard work has to be the **right** work. In the early stages of the business **you** are the most valuable resource. Therefore how you spend your time can be the most important decision. Take a moment and ask yourself: 'What is the most valuable work I should be doing this week?'

You need to start thinking like a great entrepreneur. People sometimes make the mistake of behaving and even spending like a wealthy entrepreneur, but how the great entrepreneurs behaved at the stage you are at now is the important area to analyse. At this stage, and usually later, they were extremely thrifty, wanting every penny to work in their business. The secret of real success is not in the eyes of others. Entrepreneurs are motivated less by external measures such as status and material possessions than by internal satisfactions. They can become famous for achieving wealth, but often this is a side-effect to their motivations.

THE QUALITIES NEEDED

An entrepreneur:

- Has to think of new ideas and deliver them to a market at a profit
- Has to lead their team against established competition with minimal resources
- Has to raise finance without a track record, collateral or internal experts
- Has to constantly stake their personal reputation and give guarantees
- Has to pay their staff and only pay themselves when it is prudent to do so
- Has to be prepared to lose everything if things go wrong
- Is personally threatened when the bank or a creditor puts on pressure
- Has to be harder, more flexible and more streetwise than in their previous corporate life
- Has to be good at multitasking, as initially they will have to do everything
- Has to take full responsibility for whatever happens

Progress now

Who is more successful, a millionaire or a billionaire?

_____

That depends on what their objectives were and if they are happy. This means that the answer might be neither of the above.

Being a successful entrepreneur is about improving society, adding things that were not there before. This includes personal wealth accumulation, but if that was your only target you are nothing more than a miser. The wealth of money is nothing compared with the wealth of being totally free to think, create and innovate at will, and to the knowledge that you have added value to society. An entrepreneur is an innovator, inspirer, leader and creator who adds to the lives of customers, staff and shareholders. An entrepreneur's life is full of excitement, energy, fun, friends and job satisfaction.

ENTREPRENEUR 1: MILLIONAIRE OR BILLIONAIRE?

Are you the next **Bill Gates**? Do you want to be? If you had his financial wealth, what would you do with it? Your answers will give an insight to your values and motivations. Think big, believe that you can do it, research your plans thoroughly, and perfect your formula for making money and how you intend to grow it. How, for example, will you finance such massive growth and in what timescale? There are always options: franchising, venture capital, partnering with a major company. These all need to be worked through to find the most appropriate choice.

You need a vision of the future, and to think long term. **John D. Rockefeller** rose above his competitors by seeing the importance of economies of scale and how they could operate in his industry (oil). Like many of the great entrepreneurs, he was obsessed with efficiency and control of costs.

You can start small and grow in reaction to your market. **Michael Marks**, for example, started retailing his goods working from home, personally knocking on doors and standing on street corners. This led to market trading, then a shop, then another shop: Marks and Spencer. His famous phrase, 'Don't ask the price, it is a penny', did not come from marketing genius but because he could not speak English when he started. A simple sign on his stall solved any problems, and made life easier for potential customers. Yet this simplicity continued for a long time in the company, showing how much easier it is to run a business that has simple principles and focus.

To help you develop your thinking, read the biographies of famous entrepreneurs (see page 250). Make them your role models and personal coaches. Their ideas, beliefs, values, strategies, techniques, passions and motivations are all clear.

ENTREPRENEUR 2: LIFESTYLE BUSINESS – SMALL IS BEAUTIFUL

When you plan to remain small you can cover for each other, work as a close-knit team, and management is relatively straight-forward. Once you have a secure client base, profits can be high and the lifestyle can be thoroughly satisfying. You also have a capital asset that you can sell, should you wish to.

Staff allow efficiencies in terms of delegating specialist tasks. They also mean responsibilities and need managing. You need to make sure that your productivity whilst training, managing and motivating is not compromised. Employees are not capitalists – they are just selling their labour for a monthly bill which you have to pay. For most, loyalty will be dependent on your paying them, although staff have been known to forgo salary when the pressure was on. These are rare, special individuals. Your challenge as a business leader is to ensure that the value that employees add is more than you are paying them. You have a very strong direct effect on their productivity. You can choose them, train, lead and motivate them to give their best. Your staff are stakeholders, dedicating a large chunk of their life to making it work.

ENTREPRENEUR 3: TEA FOR TWO OR THREE?

There are many advantages to partnership – not being alone being a major one. There are, however, some ground rules. When partners are not equal, even for good reason, sooner or later this will lead to conflict. The strength of any partnership should be the ideas generated by **all** the partners. If one of the partners considers his or her ideas better, conflict will arise. Partners have to have the same objectives for the business. If one is motivated purely by profit and another by achieving excellence and leadership in a product line, at some point their objectives will be divergent not convergent.

If you want a lifestyle business, you will want to keep the whole equity. If profit is your main motive, your interest will be in maximizing the value of your shareholdings in the future. This formula in itself does not suggest that you maintain a majority: would you prefer to own 100 per cent of all your researched ideas, or 30 per cent with an experienced partner and £500,000 of venture capital in the bank? With the latter financial headstart, that 30 per cent is likely to be worth more in five years' time than the 100 per cent.

ENTREPRENEUR 4: FREELANCER

Self-employment, or starting something whilst you are still in full-time employment, can be a good first step as an entrepreneur. You have broken the corporate chains and you are your own boss. You are, though, dependent at this stage on earned income from your own labour. To get rich and secure, you need to earn from things other than your labour. If you are ill for two weeks or take a holiday, the business will be closed. You are limited by the highest rate you can charge and the maximum number of hours you can work.

This, however, might be the lifestyle you want. You are your own boss, you do not have the responsibility of others, and you can be creative in your own way.

At this level, greater efficiency can be made by delegating as much as possible. For example, employ a part-time bookkeeper on an hourly rate. Their cost should be a lot lower than your charge-out rate. You must cost everything you do by the hour. Anything that is less than your charge-out rate is a contender for subcontracting.

If you wish to progress as a business, you need to do at least one of two things. The first is to make products relative to your expertise. Alternatively, you can expand, which means taking on board more resources (staff). The advantage of this is that you can wait until you are overwhelmed with work then grow from a position of strength.

ENTREPRENEUR 5: INVENTOR/ARTIST

This category of entrepreneur includes people that are not necessarily running companies at all. They are included because of their enterprise in creating something new that has commercial potential. They have the potential to turn their creativity into a substantial passive income source. In fact, many inventors go on to run companies, but this is not essential.

You may be a potential inventor, working on a product that will do something really special and in demand. **James Dyson** developed a wheelbarrow with a ball instead of a wheel. He went on to develop a new system for a vacuum cleaner. His challenging of the existing ways of doing things is an inspiration to us all. If this is the sort of entrepreneur that inspires and motivates you, you need to know a great deal about patents. You also need to consider not only whom your invention would benefit but also whom it would threaten. Does your invention render a current product obsolete? If so, the current manufacturers are most definitely threatened. They have a lot of power to protect their interests. One option, of course, is to take your invention to that big company. It has resources for finance, marketing, development and testing.

RICHARD LOWDEN

Richard is founder and managing director of Eurodrive Car Rental Ltd, a franchising group with 85 branches throughout the UK.

AM: What is your career background?

RL: I was inspired by my father, who was a very successful businessman, and by the career of Richard Branson. My first enterprise was when my father was closing down a pottery with a warehouse full of products. I told him that I would sell them for him, and did so to retailers such as garden centres and direct to the public via car boot sales. I was 13 years old. I had also worked in my sister's riding school, where I learnt a great deal about the administrative side of running a business. I was motivated to become an entrepreneur by an overwhelming passion for success.

I could not wait to leave school and worked initially in a sales capacity. My final employee position was with a major car rental company. It was here that I saw tremendous scope for improvement. I thoroughly researched every aspect of the industry. Even the name Eurodrive was based upon where I wanted to be in ten years. I left work and persuaded four investors to back me. I also negotiated contracts with Ford, Vauxhall and Peugeot, each of which were over £1 million deals. The year was 1993, and I had an overwhelming challenge to deliver what I had promised.

I intended to be a franchise group and open branches all around the UK. My philosophy is that a franchisee is the customer and I did not want the potential conflict of interest with company-owned outlets. The first franchise was going to be the hardest. I learnt to take franchises in as groups which overcame the initial 'nobody wanting to be first' obstacle.

My major problem was getting people to take me seriously at 22 years of age. I never gave up. I never rested on my laurels. I never took no for an answer.

A few years later we were firmly established and I was in the position to make attractive offers to the investors for their shares. The market is always changing and you cannot control it, so you have to predict and prepare for those changes. Now, with 85 operations, the company is funding its own growth and still returning growing profits. I have had attractive offers to sell, but I intend to make it the most recognized, best-quality car rental company on an international basis.

Our website is an interesting case. Our statistics showed that we were getting a vast quantity of requests for quotes but only a very small percentage of the subsequent bookings. We made one simple change, offering surfers the option of having their quote e-mailed to them, making it simple to order. There was a dramatic, overnight change in orders – a small fortune was created just by this one seemingly minor improvement.

I have also found that a high level of integrity is important. We always have been transparent to our customers and there are no hidden extras when you rent a car from us. Simple, straightforward, honest. We think of our franchisees as customers. I demand exceptional service. If I cannot find it, we set it up in-house.

AM: How do you define success?

RL: Success is a measure other people give you. For me it will be when we are acknowledged as the world's leading car rental company.

AM: What is the secret of success of an entrepreneur?

RL: The ability to never give up. To take any form of rejection or knockback as a lesson.

AM: What advice would you give somebody starting out?

RL: 1 Research what you are going to do thoroughly, being careful of people not telling you the truth.

2 Whatever funding you think you need, double it. Cash is paramount.

3 When you hit problems, deal with them.

4 Make sure your credit is good.

5 Surround yourself with people that are talented in areas you are not.

AM: How do you spot an opportunity?

RL: Keep your eyes open all of the time.

AM: What would you have done differently if you could go back in time?

RL: Nothing. Every mistake I made I learnt from and progressed.

AM: How do you motivate yourself when things don't go to plan?

RL: I ask myself how I can turn this to my advantage.

SUMMARY

Be all that you can dream and choose the right business for you.

Progress now

Which type of entrepreneur are you going to be? Tick all that strongly appeal.

- [ ] Self-employed – one man/woman band
- [ ] Independent consultant
- [ ] Corporate entrepreneur
- [ ] Web-based shop
- [ ] Buying a current business
- [ ] Lifestyle business
- [ ] Major multinational company
- [ ] Creator
- [ ] Artist
- [ ] Inventor
- [ ] Innovator

	Financial freedom
	Very serious wealth
	Network marketer
	Franchisee
	Franchisor
	Management buy-out
	Management buy-in

In three sentences, in the light of the above, define your dream exactly.

_____

_____

_____

_____

_____

_____

CHAPTER 3
Seeing Opportunities

Entrepreneurs are simply those who understand that there is little difference between obstacle and opportunity and are able to turn both to their advantage.

VICTOR KIAM

Being an entrepreneur is like being a policeman – you are never off duty.

SIMON MCBETH

WHAT SHALL I DO?

The question of what you want to do must be adapted to what people want to buy. You may live in Oxford and dream of your own yachting supplies shop, but do you have a market? Work is ultimately about doing something for somebody else. The real trick is to marry what people need to what you have a passion for and capability in supplying. Remember: if you get the marketing right, selling will be easy.

You can become self-employed, take on a franchise, buy a business, join a network marketing company, become a corporate entrepreneur, invent a new device or launch something new. Opportunity spotting is not just about getting an initial idea: it is a way of life. It covers every aspect and process of your business, all the time. Even after you have just improved a process, you should immediately start looking for opportunities to improve it further. We will now explore some of these options so you can decide which is for you.

Here are a few examples of where you may look for opportunities:

- A new product or service
- Enhancement of an existing product
- A new market for an existing product
- A new application for an existing product
- A source of grants or awards
- Better arrangements with suppliers
- Better promotion and advertising
- Greater efficiency of ordering
- New contact sources

Progress now

What three areas of opportunity would be valuable to you right now?

_____

_____

_____

Which of the following do you think have a good chance of success?

1 A watch that you can speak into with a country name: it will give you the time and other information about that country.

2 An alarm for parents so that when one of their young children is over 50 yards away they are warned and given a direction indication.

3 An IT professional setting up a recruitment agency specializing in IT people.

4 An open training seminar called 'How to overcome shyness'.

5 A bathroom mirror with a slight angle to make people look thinner than they are.

6 A wool shop in a residential estate.

You may think the answers to the above are obvious. Actually you would be right; yet being obviously wrong does not stop people from blindly following their dream. If you answered 'It depends' to any project, what would you need to know to establish its viability?

CONFUSION TO CLARITY

What words come to your mind when you say 'entrepreneur'?
Here is a list that was produced during a training session.

Creative	Endeavour	Gamble
Money	Lending	Negotiator
Ideas	Project	Challenge
Opportunity	Risk	Possibility
Profit	Venture	Niche
Independence	Ambitious	Marketeer
Competition	Drive	Promotion
Arrogance	Enthusiasm	Wheeler-dealer
Change agent	Imagination	Catalyst
Millionaire	Big picture	Initiative
Teleworker	Dream	Vision
Freedom	Inventor	Selling
Inspiration		

Progress now

Circle the words above that interest you.

What key personal qualities do you need to be a successful entrepreneur?

_____

_____

What are your personal qualities?

_____

_____

What could you improve?

_____

_____

What action are you going to take to achieve that?

_____

_____

ACTING ON INSPIRATION

Have you ever travelled abroad and had the following interesting experiences?

- ◊ Noticing something in that country which is better than at home: you cannot imagine why it does not exist where you come from.

- ◊ Seeing something that is worse in the country visited than at home: why don't they do it your way?

- ◊ Seeing something quite different: you cannot figure out if it is better or worse than at home, but it has given you ideas.

That is the entrepreneur in you trying to come out.

This is how entrepreneurs think. They observe, analyse and constantly ask themselves questions. It is easy to get it wrong, but that gives you valuable information to help you get it right next time. In addition, when you get it right, the payoffs are truly exciting. The process of being an entrepreneur is an adventure in itself. Is your work at the moment an exciting adventure? It should be.

You need to maximize the use of resources, relating this all the time to potential sales and profit. Look around you: what is there that could be used in a different way to more effect? What resources can you see that are being underemployed? This is how many people decide to turn their garage into a cheap and convenient office!

THE OPPORTUNIST

It is a myth that entrepreneurs simply find an idea then run with it. In reality, you need to be constantly looking for new opportunities and constantly updating your original one. Ideas in themselves are common: the real trick is to turn ideas into commercial reality. Entrepreneurs are not in the business of saying 'I told you somebody would invent a product that would do that.' You have to make things happen through your **belief**, **conviction**, **determination**, **enthusiasm**, **commitment** and **practical ability**.

The four steps to spot opportunities:

1   Ask the magic six questions:

   a)   What or who has presented a potential opportunity to me today?

   b)   From the people that I met today, what need do they seem to have?

   c)   What have I kept hearing from people over the past week?

   d)   What is happening out there right now? What is there an increased need for?

e) What would people buy in great quantity if it existed now?

f) What service or product would I buy today if it existed?

2 Stick a copy of the six questions on your wall and read them at the start of each day.

3 Observe and listen as you go through the day.

4 Wait. The questions are in your unconscious, working away. You have trained your mind to focus automatically on opportunities. Soon ideas will start flowing. Soon you will realize that commercial opportunities are presented in front of your nose on a daily basis.

The four steps to turn opportunities into profit:

1 Establish a market price and how to reach it.

2 Determine how much it would cost to produce an initial stock of the product or deliver the service.

3 Work out the finances.

4 Remember: think big but get some feedback first with limited risk. All results are valuable feedback, so keep listening.

KEVIN UPHILL

Kevin is co-founder and managing director of Avondale Group Ltd, a UK specialist in the sale, merger and acquisition of small to medium sized commercial businesses.

AM: What is your career background?

KU: I was employed as a business development consultant and I was interested, with my father, to buy a business transfer franchise. We took advice from the Training and Enterprise Council and they suggested that with our profiles we really ought to start our own business. I believed in taking expert advice right from the start, so that is what we did. I was motivated to be an entrepreneur because I saw it as the biggest challenge, a way to control my own destiny and the only way I could see myself making a million.

My father and I had many complementary skills. However, looking back, we were both arrogant and did not really know very much about running a business. In the first five years we made the mistake of working in the business and not on the business itself. We sell small and medium-sized enterprises as a brokerage.

This meant that we deal with successful entrepreneurs who are in a position to realize a capital gain on a daily basis.

After we were established and profitable, I was motivated to make some serious money. We asked ourselves some interesting questions to develop our business into something that would make us a lot of money. Specifically we asked the question: 'How could we develop it so that it pays us a great deal more?' We also saw a potential capital gain as a key objective. As our business meant dealing with successful entrepreneurs, we had a great deal of experience available to us from which to learn.

We decided to grow with an emphasis on installing some very efficient systems and processes. We developed a network of offices around the country, largely on retained earnings, with a programme of continuous improvement. We asked, and continue to ask, the question 'How can we make this better?', on every single component of the business at every single point of time.

I was also influenced at the time by the idea that if you cannot be the first in your sector, make your own sector. I saw James Dyson's success as an ideal example of this. So I clarified our market niche within selling small to medium-sized businesses and our consultancy approach. We stopped dealing with high street retailers and touched nothing under at least £50K profit. We also recruited very high quality people capable and credible in advising people who, after all, had successfully built up a profitable business. We also invested in training. Our income went up by a factor of five following the enhancements, and we are still growing.

AM: How do you define success?

KU: Health, happiness, fun and balance.

AM: What is the secret of success of an entrepreneur?

KU: To be aware of all the components that make up a business and be receptive to improving them.

AM: What advice would you give somebody starting out?

KU: 1 Listen attentively.

2 Be aware of your own strengths and weaknesses.

3 Do not believe your own dream. Look at it from an outside perspective and be objective.

4 Work smart before hard.

5 Make business your hobby and make sure it is fun.

AM: How do you spot an opportunity?

KU: Get a raw idea, work out the costs and profits in your head and only get enthusiastic if it has a strong chance of generating a good cash return.

AM: What would you have done differently if you could go back in time?

KU: I would have got more knowledge on marketing and sales issues.

AM: How do you motivate yourself when things don't go to plan?

KU: Winning counts, but if you have done your best, it's fine. Learn from the experience and get going.

YOUR LUCKY DAY

Opportunities come in many shapes and sizes . . . and they keep coming. They are like trains leaving a station: if you miss one there will be another one leaving soon. Who knows, it may be that missing a train puts a once-in-a-lifetime opportunity in front of you: whilst having an unplanned coffee, you may notice something interesting about the people in the café, something that you realize would be really useful to them whilst waiting for a train. Alternatively, perhaps you get talking to someone at the same table and the conversation triggers an idea, or maybe both of you together can offer something that you could not alone. Many partnerships have been built this way.

What, in your industry, is outdated? What is happening that everybody takes for granted, but in fact no longer has a use? Companies are very quick to make people redundant. They are less quick to make things, processes or ways of doing things redundant, particularly if the management team's power base is their experience of doing it that old, redundant way. That is the opportunity for entrepreneurs to enter and update things. Turning a large company around can be like turning a supertanker around in a harbour. The entrepreneur can move more quickly and is not hampered by outdated ways of doing things, or outdated people resisting change.

In a changing world, the consumer will be looking for new things all the time. Needs change and things go in and out of fashion.

How entrepreneurs make their own luck:

- 🐾 They look and listen for opportunities constantly.
- 🐾 They believe that in everything that happens there is opportunity somewhere.
- 🐾 They think ahead and plan for every contingency.
- 🐾 They get in tune with what people would pay money for. They then make this their focus.

FAILURE . . . AND OTHER OPPORTUNITIES

You need to have the ability to learn from failure: your failures and, more importantly, those of others. Information and opportunities are coming at you from all directions non-stop. The trick is to delete the vast majority that do not hold opportunity, so you can see clearly what is left. As **Richard Lowden** of Eurodrive Car Rental says: **'Every time I receive a setback, I immediately ask myself: how can I turn this to my advantage? All others do is focus on solving the immediate problem.'**

Often a failure can be the inspiration for a new launch. Sometimes that failure can be the rejection of an idea you have and your employer rejects. The idea fails before it is given a chance. All venture capitalists have tales of ideas they rejected that others took on board and which then became a great success. The real skill lies in finding ways to make your ideas work commercially.

ENTREPLOYEE

You must be prepared to get out of the 'salary mentality' and sacrifice the short term for a considerably better long term. Many new entrepreneurs measure how they are doing against their previous salary. This is understandable, but it has no relevance and takes your thinking away from a useful, productive focus. You will need patience and belief in yourself to keep going.

This shows a typical employee over eight weeks:

month's work → salary → month's work → salary

Here it is again, a bit closer:

bad month → salary → good month → same salary

A job is a business with one client, with no scope to expand, in which any capital gain or goodwill you develop is for the profit of that client. If you do well in the year you could earn 20 per cent more in year two and that would be an exceptional success. An entrepreneur looks for leverage of 200 per cent in the first year.

WHY DO YOU WANT TO BE A VERY SUCCESSFUL ENTREPRENEUR?

People who have been employees for a long while have got used to being motivated by their need for status: company cars, size of office, salary grade etc. Entrepreneurs lead a company **and** roll their sleeves up, take full pride in every aspect and will do any task that needs doing. For example, if **Michael Marks** of Marks & Spencer noticed a mess in a store, he would clear it up himself.

Employees are rewarded by being given material bonuses that are visible signs of their success. This trains their unconscious mind to search for more recognition. So they buy expensive clothes, the latest hi-fi etc. To be an entrepreneur, you have to learn financial discipline. Make a decision to find out exactly what you want to do . . . and do it. The threat and fear of going hungry will make you magically resourceful.

Venture capitalists and business angel networks are inundated by would-be entrepreneurs whose plan seems to focus on their getting a secure wage. Investors want to invest in a business, not pay you a fat salary.

Employee thinking	**Entrepreneur thinking**
I need a monthly salary	I need to make a profit
I need a good pension scheme	I need a capital gain to retire on
I want a promotion	If you want to get to the top, start there
Thank God it's Friday	God, is it Friday already?
If I qualify I can get a good job	If I set up my own business I can employ well-qualified people
I want a better job	I have a dream
What do you want me to do?	What needs doing?
I have a great idea	Here is my new product
I need a secure job	I want to be financially free
I look forward to retiring at 65	I never want to retire, but I will be able to soon
I want high status	I want to control my own destiny
I want to stay on the boss's good side	I want independence
I like to keep to my strength area	I need creativity and variety

I feel great frustration	I have incredible job satisfaction
I need a fixed income	I'm expecting unlimited income
I want a higher salary	I want capital gain
I have done my best	Never give up

Progress now

Circle the above choices depending on which ones more closely describes you.

Are you ready, or do you have to make some changes? Write those changes here.

_____

_____

_____

_____

_____

WHERE DO I START?

You start by asking questions and then more questions. Questions get answers, so make sure that yours are well chosen.

WHY questions:

- Why does it happen like this?
- Why can I not get what I want?
- Why do people tolerate this?
- Why has nobody improved this?

WHAT questions:

- What assumptions are applicable here?
- What was once useful but is now redundant?
- What has changed recently?
- What is redundant here?

HOW questions:

- How can I improve this?
- How could it be done better?
- How would I have done this?
- How can I profit from this right now?

WHEN questions:

- When does this not work well?
- When will the market for this be ready?
- When was this process established?
- When will this idea be outdated?

There are many directions in which you can take an idea, and by giving it a twist you can turn it into a moneymaker. Look at the progress now box on page 63.

Welcome to how entrepreneurs find those new ideas. It is all about the type of question you ask and in what order. The random selection allows you to look at it in a way you would not normally. That is how you can see what has always been there that you never noticed before. The next point that you might have already realized is that there are infinite permutations of question sets and therefore an infinite amount of potential ways to enhance, reinvent or create a new product or service on every product. There is that much abundance of opportunity available! There are no such things as scarcity and market size.

Progress now

1   Write a dozen – three of each – of your own Why, What, How and When questions on separate pieces of paper. Shuffle the papers and turn them face down.

2   Pick four questions randomly, and write them down on a clean piece of paper.

3   Think of any product or service that you have bought in the past month.

4   Ask those four questions of the product or service until you have at least three answers to each question.

5   At the end of this exercise, ask this final question: From this new knowledge and perspective, what improvement, enhancement or new product or service comes to mind that has a market?

6   You now have the raw ingredient for a new business that already has a potential market.

THE BUCK STOPS HERE

You are the boss: this means that everything is your fault if it goes wrong. Take responsibility. This does not mean you have to be an expert on everything, or indeed anything. You can employ experts. If you don't want to be the boss you can employ someone who has more experience than you. This depends on what type of entrepreneur you have decided to be.

Creative entrepreneurs often inspire leadership, but when it comes to day-to-day management they would sooner delegate. However, there are many different leadership styles that work. There is not one magic formula, although you are setting the culture for the organization that you are building. There are many books on leadership and management. This area is well covered. This book addresses specific challenges that occur to entrepreneur-based companies, and how to deal with them.

The entrepreneur typically is stretching the resources to meet the monthly payroll. Many entrepreneurs have had to maintain and motivate their staff even when they could not pay them. That is leadership!

PENNIES FROM HEAVEN

Contrary to popular belief, successful entrepreneurs live frugally, wanting every penny to be invested in their business. They now control their lives: they have made a decision to determine their own destiny. They don't need material, external consumer products to give them status or to make them feel good when low. They are already free and getting freer. Statistics show that the wealthiest people in the country are not the highest spenders.

If you have been in employment for a while, your natural entrepreneurial instincts may have been eroded and you are in the rut of getting things you want by making money to pay for them: reward and pressure are directly related to real success or failure. This system programs you to avoid failure and to seek more reward. If you want to be an entrepreneur, harden up and give up your credit card lifestyle. If this means you go hungry, then go hungry. In practice you won't: your unconscious is always seeking to protect you and will focus on taking positive action. You need to get in the habit of short-term pressure leading to longer-term gratification.

TRANSFORMATIONS

Large companies have specialist departments, big budgets and a range of resources. The entrepreneur has to source things without access to experts, dedicated staff etc. For example, if a start-up entrepreneur wants to run training for six staff, they probably won't have a training room, flipchart or budget. In addition, if they train in the day the company will be closed for business. These sorts of practical day-to-day challenge have to be met by thinking on your feet. An entrepreneur would typically network to find a trainer willing to do a favour, find someone who has a room they are not using and ask around as to who has a flipchart.

Progress now

Invent a new word. That's right – invent one.

Did you know that there are thousands of words in hundreds of different languages that have no equivalent translation in English? In fact if you are a native English speaker the syntax, order of words, spelling and grammar will set you up for a certain way of thinking, thus limiting you. Different languages also have different non-verbal languages. Watch people talking to each other in a swimming pool and it is possible to tell their nationality from a distance. It is also possible to know what they are talking about. Each variation represents a different way of looking at things, and thus a potential insight to lucrative commercial opportunities.

WE CAN HAVE AND BE HEROES

Walt Disney showed all the qualities of an entrepreneur: creativity, adding value to society, fun and freedom for the mind to wander. Disney's drive did not come from the potential of making big money: that was a side-effect that took a long time coming. He and other great entrepreneurs were motivated by many different things. What they had in common was an obsessive passion for what they wanted. They took some very big knocks along the way, some even going bankrupt more than once before achieving success. Entrepreneurs need a great reservoir of inner strength.

Progress now

Who are your three favourite entrepreneurs?

_____

_____

_____

Read more about them: this will help you to determine what type of entrepreneur you want to be.

JOINING THE CLUB

When someone can do something exceptionally well, to them by definition it is usually easy. This tends to mean that they underestimate the value of that talent. What are you outstanding at? Who would have a use for that talent? You must work to your strengths. If you need other skills, employ them or contract them out. Too many books on entrepreneurship cover all the areas of business: accounting, marketing, personnel etc. If you try to learn everything you need to know, you will explode. Do what you are good at, recognize what you are not good at and what is needed, and bring it in. Even when small, business is still a team sport.

Progress now

What do you have a passion for?

_____

_____

What do you believe in?

_____

_____

What annoys you?

_____

_____

What do others say you have a talent for?

_____

_____

THE PURIST

As any entrepreneur capitalizes on opportunity, you must know where most of your revenue is coming from and focus your attention there. Once started, you must build an organization that can exploit effectively the opportunity you spotted. You need the ability to see a market trend and act on it.

Money magnet questions:

- Now what?
- Is my idea good?
- Is it original?
- Is it worth anything?
- Will it sell?
- What is nearest to money?
- What is most lucrative long term?
- What will people pay for?
- What do people not only want but also need?
- What would my favourite entrepreneur do if he or she were me?

ONLY YOU CAN DECIDE

Progress now

Tick the statements that are true for you.

- [ ] A traditional job would not provide me with the independence and financial opportunities that I seek.

- [ ] I have always wanted to run my own business.

- [ ] I had a great idea last year and somebody else did it this year.

- [ ] I know what I want to do and how, but am fearful of meeting my monthly bills.

- [ ] I see businesses around me and know I could make more profit from them.

- [ ] I would like to retire before I am 50.

- [ ] Nobody where I work wants to listen to my ideas.

- [ ] I have a talent for noticing what others don't seem to notice.

Many entrepreneurs have a real talent in getting something created and off the ground. Often, however, this is the point where professional managers need to take over more and more. By recruiting people from quality company backgrounds you will get on board the processes, procedures and organization that your business increasingly needs. Most entrepreneurs hate this sort of work and want to go on creating. Avoid people from your own industry, though, as evidence shows that they will introduce to you the way your big competitor does things. To get ahead of your competitors from a smaller base you need to do things **better**.

SUMMARY

It is important to know what type of entrepreneur you really want to be. As things progress, what role do you see for yourself? You must work where your passion and talent lie to really achieve great things. Don't be dragged into the role of MD if day-to-day management is not your interest. Don't be afraid of appointing somebody over you, who is more experienced in that role. If you are an inventor, keep inventing – let somebody else work up the value of your shares.

Progress now

Write down three opportunities that you can see a market for right now.

_____

_____

_____

Which one do you have an overwhelming belief in and passion for?

CHAPTER 4

Maintaining Passion, Persistence and Personal Power

In desperation you can achieve anything.

VIJAY DHIR

I have always been bored with just making money. I have wanted to do things; I wanted to build things.

WALT DISNEY

FEELING FANTASTIC

Success is an internal feeling of well-being – it is not something external. Having things does not indicate success. Entrepreneurship is all about finding out what people need and supplying it. It therefore gives you a great opportunity to raise your self-esteem and self-worth.

Like any determined pursuit, it is clear that the mark of a winner in the entrepreneur business is determined when things are going wrong. If there is a clear long-term vision and determination, anything in the short term will be seen as a temporary setback along the path to success. If your vision is more short term, the pictures in your mind will appear overwhelming and dominate your focus and emotions.

WHEN THE GOING GETS TOUGH YOU HAVE TO GET TOUGHER

During a tough period you may be tempted to give up and take a regular job. Most people who start their own business focus on it all going well. Those that focus on its potential to go wrong tend to not start. The biggest threat to your business is not your competitors or market but your losing confidence and belief.

If the going gets tough, it is time to get creative and even more determined. This does not mean sticking rigidly to something that does not work. It means making it work whatever changes have to be made. Use your brain to get out of difficult situations. Your brain does not work that effectively if it gets itself into a negative state. Therefore, it is important to maintain your confidence.

THE POSITIVE BENEFITS OF NEGATIVE THINKING

There is a myth that entrepreneurs are less concerned about security than are their employee counterparts. This can be true, but often entrepreneurs just see it differently. They want their security to be under their own control, which suggests that they have a stronger need for security.

Entrepreneurs are more negative than positive. In fact they spend a great deal of time considering what will happen if it all goes wrong. They focus on dealing with this negative and on applying their positive energy to it.

Progress now

Think of five things in your business, or planned business, that could go wrong in the next 12 months: recession, offices flooded, lawsuit, competitors cutting prices, not raising enough finance, cash flow crisis, problem finding suitable staff etc.

1 _____

2 _____

3 _____

4 _____

5 _____

Now think of actions you can take now to prepare for each event.

1 _____

2 _____

3 _____

4 _____

5 _____

Now think of an action you can take for each of the above scenarios that would turn it into an opportunity for you.

1 _____

2 _____

3 _____

4 _____

5 _____

ROLLERCOASTER TO ROCKET

To anyone who has studied the stock markets or raised risk capital it is clear that investors, however well informed, will react according to two emotions: fear and greed. To be successful you must control both your emotions. You must be as productive after a long run of bad experience as you are after a run of good.

Most entrepreneurs have taken very big risks. Many of them lost everything then started again. They were following a dream with passion and determination. Those that are focused just on accumulating money have a tendency to avoid risk as soon as they have something to lose, thus — ironically — limiting their potential. The **risk takers** love passionately what they are doing. The **risk avoiders** love money passionately, and losing even a small amount makes them very unhappy.

So if you are passionate about what you do, when the going gets tough put your head down and work harder, learning and changing as you go. Your work is the source of your results, and if you focus on where you are going, you cannot also dwell on problems that are day by day moving further into your past.

AMBITION TO ACTION

Be in a hurry, but walk before you run.

Ambition can be a dangerous energy. It can drive you forward at too fast a pace. Go as fast as possible but no faster.

Most average entrepreneurs have trained themselves to react quickly to anything that happens, to maintain their emotional state and to take action. The excellent entrepreneurs, however, have the advantage of anticipating things before they happen and taking preventative measures.

Ask yourself the following questions:

- If I was to have an absolutely wonderful idea right now, what would it be?
- If Bill Gates was a director of my business, what changes would he make?
- Is every part of me 100 per cent behind and believing in this idea?

The very factors that give you pause before starting can help you to start. For most, avoiding problems makes them take more action than does the incentive of reward.

DONKEY DERBY

There is an old saying that if you want to get a donkey to move you have two choices. You can entice him forward with the temptation of a juicy carrot, or you can hit him with a stick. Your motion is determined by the carrots and sticks operating on you. If you don't control the system, your unconscious and the environment will generate a system for you.

Sticks:

- The realization that if you are a failure you will have to live with it
- Losing everything, including your house
- Unemployment
- Letting your family down

Carrots:

- Financial security
- Job satisfaction
- Realizing your dreams
- Incredible house, holidays, cars all paid for in cash

- All the joys that success brings
- The rise in self-esteem and well-being
- Freedom to do whatever you want
- Being your own boss

SENSEI PAUL ELLIOTT

Sensei Paul founded, runs and is expanding a group of karate schools around the south of England.

AM: What is your career background?

PE: I was originally a trainee electrician and later worked for a smaller company. In 1980 I opened my first karate club in Sussex with a small group whilst maintaining full-time employment. It was not until ten years later that I was really fed up working for somebody else. I really wanted to be my own boss and work at something I really loved and found worthwhile. In fact, teaching and helping others were major motivations in themselves. I get a real buzz from teaching, and I am teaching my hobby. I was thinking about this at the time when my company was bought by a larger group, which also made the job less appealing. Initially I had a small income from the club and also did some freelance work as an electrical expert.

I realized from the start that I had to sell myself, and worked non-stop at all sorts of ideas to promote the club. I had to inform people of its existence to get them there, to maintain interest to keep them coming and to spread a good reputation. I had posters put up, leaflets distributed, took out newspaper advertising and visited adult education centres. I took a lot of action to promote myself and offered a variety of services. I have now opened other clubs around the south and am looking for instructors further afield.

In 1997 I opened a shop with a partner that turned out to be a disaster for me. I was left responsible for debt that was not really mine. I could have pursued it legally but I knew that my energy was more productively utilized in building a karate school. Negative energy needs to be let go and replaced with positive attitude.

I am always looking at new things. I set up a separate club for children and used teaching methods that were more applicable. In fact, I have many children that I have trained to black belt. I am developing a web page with one of my members and producing videos with another. I am also developing healing courses, which is another side of the martial arts, using the chi energy.

How I run the club with my team is very different. I do a great deal of research and also put many variations in the syllabus. This helps me maintain my interest and this attracts people to the club. I teach skills and techniques, for example, in how to talk your way out of a fight or calm a situation down. You have to be patient with a business. I set up a new club once and had only one client for three months. Then it grew to twenty!

Wado Ryu means 'the way of peace' and this is the focus of the discipline. For example, pressure points can be used in self-defence techniques. They can also be used in healing techniques such as acupressure. Karate is all about control of internal energies. I use the term 'energy vampires' to describe negative people, situations and objects that can drain your energy.

AM: How do you define success?

PE: Being happy at what you do. If you suddenly lost all your material possessions, would you still be happy? I would.

AM: What advice would you give somebody starting out?

PE: 1 You have got to take a gamble and trust that you can do it.

2 Be wary of taking on a partner.

3 Don't get in a rut doing things the same way. Try something else.

4 Don't do everything yourself. Look for advice.

5 Don't worry about security. The companies that I had secure jobs with have all gone now.

6 Minimize the risks. Take any safeguards. I have medical insurance, for example.

AM: How do you motivate yourself when things go wrong?

PE: One door closes . . . others open.

AM: How do you spot an opportunity?

PE: Ideas just come, particularly during quiet times or meditation. I constantly ask myself what to do next. If you try to think of ideas they might never come; if you have a clear mind, ideas come.

PERSONAL POWER

There can be two reasons for your feeling low. You may be focusing on some bad news. Or you may feel low for no apparent reason. You then search for things that are negative, then dwell on them and maintain your low feeling for even longer.

The following actions will clear out this negative energy:

- **Focus on the positive.** Write down five things that are really positive in your life now. Then write one page of notes on each and reread them every morning, updating them when appropriate. Read a different book every month on business or personal development or biographies of those you admire.

- **Keep busy.** Taking action forces the mind to focus on the positive. In addition, action is what creates good news, so get to it as quickly as possible.

- **Exercise.** This flushes the system out and generates a positive flow of energy.

- **Replace coffee, tea, fizzy drinks and alcohol with water.** You will be surprised how this will wash away that low feeling and those negative thoughts.

FAST FORWARD

Make a simple analysis of the verb tenses that you use by noting down in three columns every verb you say (or write): past, present and future. Total up each column to see where your focus is. Most successful entrepreneurs use predominantly the future tense, then the present and finally the past. Try to make a point of using the future tense. It will improve your outlook, idea generation and confidence.

Progress now

Think of a famous entrepreneur that you admire. Listen to a TV or radio programme on which they appear, or read their autobiography. Track their use of verb tenses, as above. A pattern will soon emerge.

DESIRE . . . ASPIRE . . . RETIRE

Most professional recruiters know that the most placeable candidate is the one with the most desire to be placed. Desire is the energy that make things happen and leads to success, whatever comes in the way.

Desires to be a real entrepreneur are often in conflict with desires for avoiding risk, for instant gratification and for security. The desires that hold you back are of two kinds:

🖎 **Fear.** Fears about everything going wrong, losing your house, not getting your job back, the unknown. Lack of self-confidence is in this category.

🖎 **Short-term gratification.** Increasingly, society is being hypnotized by the promise of instant consumption. These short-term hungers are never satisfied: you just keep wanting more and more. You have to take control of your desires to grow into your potential as an entrepreneur.

Progress now

What desires do you have that are keeping you from your dreams?

_____

_____

_____

What weaknesses do you have that are keeping you from your dreams?

_____

_____

_____

From the above decide what action you have to take.

You need to reprogram your habits so that they automatically achieve your goals for you.

Progress now

Write down all the habits that you would like to change.
Include those that you know are a waste of money, time or
other resources: smoking, drinking, watching too much TV,
getting up late, spending to make yourself feel good, avoiding
exercise, worry, talking yourself into a negative state.

_____

_____

_____

_____

Now write down habits that you would like to cultivate: regular
exercise, thrift, opportunity spotting, opportunity developing,
being positive when you need to be.

_____

_____

_____

Here is a formula to stop a bad habit:

1 Do something different every time it comes up.
2 Remind yourself of your goals and dreams.

Here is a formula for forming a habit:

1 Think of something you love doing. Take those feelings and now think of the new habit, focusing on the long-term benefits. Bring those images that come to mind closer and closer.
2 Do it consciously 7 times in a row.
3 Now do it 7 more.
4 It is now in your unconscious.

CHAPTER 5
Going To Plan?

> **Singleness of purpose is one of the chief essentials for success in life, no matter what may be one's aim.**
>
> JOHN D. ROCKEFELLER

> **Once a day is gone you can never get it back again.**
>
> RICHARD LOWDEN

TYPES OF COMPANY

One of the first decisions before you set sail is the form of legal entity you will operate under. Depending on what country you are in, there are various forms of trading. **Incorporating** is the favourite choice, and usually the best option as this gives you limited liability for your debts, making you and the company separate legal entities. In other words, a creditor can sue only the company for its money and not the shareholders or directors. Of course, finance companies, banks and suppliers often seek personal guarantees or cash deals because of this. A **partnership** can exist because your accounts are not in the public domain. You are technically liable, though, for anything any partner signs in the partnership name. Some firms, like accountants and lawyers, have to be partnerships. A **sole trader** is just yourself but you need not trade under your own name.

THINKING ABOUT THE FUTURE

Bill Gates famously visualized a PC in every home. **Walt Disney** visualized Disneyland clearly in his mind's eye then endeavoured tirelessly to make it a reality. When they had these ideas they were laughed at. If someone is laughing at your dreams, you are in good company.

In addition, entrepreneurs must have a clear vision of how they are going to survive and prosper in the short term. They can see potential customers going for their ideas. They can see staff being motivated by their leadership.

Most people in business tend to be good at visualization for either the short term or the long term. Entrepreneurs invariably do both. When this is not the case, successful entrepreneurs have a partner with the other skill: one of them is the strategist and the other the tactician. The strategist is often the innovator – the creator of new products and ideas. The tactician is the one that makes it happen.

The message is clear:

- Establish whether you are more naturally focused on the short or the long term. Listen to your own language patterns and refer back to things you have written. Look back at your career: what have been your key strengths and achievements? Were you best at short-term actions or long-term planning.

- If you are stronger in one direction you need to make a choice between recruiting someone with the other talent or developing that talent yourself.

PREPARING THE BUSINESS PLAN

If you are raising money, you will need to present a business plan. Business plans tend to have a fairly formal layout and people get used to reading a standardized format. Start with an **executive summary**, commonly known as the 'elevator pitch' (i.e. making your pitch as though passing someone on an elevator – you must get to the point quickly). Detail can be kept in an appendix for reference. The key aspect is the accounts. Three years' projected profit and loss account, cash flow and balance sheet will usually be required. If you are already trading, your results to date need to be included.

The next key area that will be looked at is the quality and appropriateness of the management team.

The plan needs to pre-empt any question that a potential investor reading through may ask, such as what would happen if:

1 A recession suddenly happened?
2 Your three key employees resigned and took your top client with them?

3 You were ill for six weeks?

4 The government gave you a tax audit?

5 Your bank called in an overdraft?

6 Your landlord wanted her premises back?

7 Your largest customer went into liquidation, owing you a small fortune?

Are you prepared for these eventualities? Would you know how to turn them to advantage? So many plans assume that if you throw a big enough cheque book at marketing, sales will follow. Venture after venture goes down because of this thinking.

Part of your plan will include what is called a SWOT analysis, covering key strengths, weaknesses, opportunities and threats. It gives a potential investor a synopsis of the opportunity. Type 'business plans' into an internet search engine and you will be directed to various examples which are useful as a checklist for your own enterprise. In practice, it is always prudent not to overestimate yourself or underestimate your competitors.

THE MAGIC FORMULA: S — C = P

Sales less costs equals profit.

Everything in business boils down to this simple relationship. If you want to succeed in your new business, work to increase sales relative to costs. £10 million sales with £10 million costs makes the same profit as someone who has not started yet.

In most entrepreneur-based businesses, costs literally come out of the owner's pocket. Owners are more inclined to be careful with their housekeeping. The so-called dotcom boom in the 1990s was a break from this successful pattern. As the internet was getting going, greedy investors were happy to put billions in the hands of young technical experts, few of whom had any business experience. The result was the dotcom boom, fuelled by a gold rush mentality. Internet companies got a bad name and then found it hard to raise capital. Some critics considered that these boom/bust companies were never proper companies in the first place and wrongly gave bad press to the potential of the internet start-ups.

Think of a business as a giant bucket where the taps pour in liquid gold. Your objective is to have the taps on full whilst making sure that all the leaks are plugged. Many owners rush to get more sales – turn the taps full on – to maintain the level in their leaky bucket, when what they should be doing is managing their costs more effectively – plugging the leaks. The way to start doing this is by questioning each and every one of them.

GOLDEN RULES

1 If you are going off course, don't keep drifting

The purpose of a plan is far more than to raise money. Design it to be a compass that will steer you through every eventuality. You should be constantly referring to your plan. Your time as an entrepreneur is your company's greatest asset. Staying until the ship goes down can take for ever and deny you the next opportunity. Stay focused on your long-term goal. This sometimes means abandoning the direction you are going in.

2 Keep tabs

Always know the statistics that are relevant to your business: cash in and out, sources of sales enquiries etc. To navigate your ship you have to have constant updates of a changing situation in order to make meaningful decisions.

3 Opportunity seeking is constant

You need constantly to be looking for new opportunities and improvements. Remember that a failure can be often the creative grounds for the next launch.

4 If you believe in it, launch it

Have you ever had a great idea, proudly told your friends of your innovation . . . then done nothing about it and watched somebody else make it succeed? Entrepreneurs are not looking for their friends to admire their ideas and intellect. They are looking to change the world and make a pile of cash. If you keep throwing the die, a six must come up eventually. You are allowed as many throws as you want.

ON TARGET FOR SUCCESS

Goal setting is clearly a habit of highly successful people in business and outside. Daily, weekly, monthly, yearly, five yearly . . . successes know where they are heading and increase their chances of getting there. Plan what you want to achieve long term and work backwards so that each day you are a step closer to your dreams.

The bad news is that making a lot of money as an entrepreneur comes through a great deal of hard work. The good news is that other people will do a great deal of it. Entrepreneurs always have a ready supply of people wanting to work for them.

Progress now

What are your three top long-term goals?

1 _____

2 _____

3 _____

Why? _____

What would happen if you did achieve them?

_____

What would happen if you did not achieve them?

_____

Are you totally sure you don't want to change them?

_____

Would you do whatever it takes to achieve them, even if meant sacrifices now?

_____

PAUL NUTH

Paul is an independent business owner, managing and developing an international network of distributors offering a vast range of home-delivered products.

AM: What is your own career background?

PN: I joined the Royal Navy straight from school with an interest in seeing the world and playing a range of sports. I was told I would never become an officer. In fact I reached the rank of lieutenant commander and most latterly was serving with the Australian Navy.

I felt that it was time to make a move. I was also motivated to ensure that I would be financially secure for old age. I wanted to have my own business and the real objective was to become free, financially and of control mechanisms, and to provide a good education and upbringing for my children. The idea of buying a business or a franchise did not appeal, though, and I had limited resources anyway.

It was at this time that I was introduced to one of the wealthiest men in Sydney who owned property and investments around the world. He was 63 and had been what I would call financially free since 27. He introduced me to an opportunity with an organization called IDA. I believed in taking advice on wealth only from people that had achieved it, so I listened attentively. I had found what I was looking for and I thought I could better develop the enormity of what I had seen back in Europe.

Although I started in Australia, I really got going in the UK. In the early nineties there was quite a recession and I was unemployed and got into debt to the tune of £70,000. I was on the edge of personal bankruptcy for quite a while. The ideal plan would have been to have a regular job whilst I built up my own business in my free time. In fact, within three years I had paid off this debt and had started to accumulate assets. You certainly have more choices when you have money. I was determined that lack of money would not decide where and how I spent my retirement. From there I continued to build my business whilst holding down a full-time job, recruiting more independent business owners in a system developed from the principle of network marketing.

The beauty was that IDA provided me with regular training and support from people that had started before me. They taught me how to become financially independent. My success has come from following their advice. IDA has thousands of people who need not ever work again, and I have had direct access to all this knowledge. IDA provided an environment for anybody with the will to succeed in the industry that it was formed to support. It is led and populated by people that have done it. I had the will to succeed and was keen to listen to advice from wealthy people.

You build people; they build the business. If the desire is there, anybody can learn anything, but a supportive environment helps. Whatever problems you have will pass – it's your reaction to them that matters. My results were based on duplication and leverage in a system that works. The only real resource that I needed to add was my time. IDA has effectively given me a degree in behavioural psychology and taught me how to control my motivation, be successful and overcome my fears.

I see people around me and they seem to anaesthetize themselves against thinking of the future. Every single successful person I studied had a clear dream that they focused on. I ask people, 'If you could take the rest of the year off, with no constraints on time or money, what would you do?' They find it a hard question to answer. I ask, 'Does the thought of an extra income stream appeal?' Most are caught up in selling their time for money for 40 years and know little about how wealth is accumulated. The system seems to take away their hopes of a better future.

I continually read biographies of successful people and I listen to at least five personal development tapes per week. I believe the mind is a magnificent mechanism, but you have to program it: if you do not put in content for the future it can only refer to the past. I have taken longer than expected to get where I am. I have set goals and missed them three times but eventually got there.

AM: What motivated you to be an entrepreneur?

PN: To become financially free and own my own time.

AM: How do you define success?

PN: When I totally control my time. A happy, balanced family.

AM: What is the secret of success of an entrepreneur?

PN: 1 Be willing to define and do what it takes.

    2 When you set your goal, make it non-negotiable.

    3 Do it or don't do it.

    4 You cannot build it on your own.

    5 Leverage your time.

    6 Fast is better.

7 Have fun.

8 Like baking a cake, you have to put the right ingredients in, in the right way.

AM: What advice would you give somebody starting out?

PN: 1 Determine why you are doing it and put it in writing.

2 Don't negotiate the price.

3 Be willing to work.

4 Enjoy the journey.

5 Act with integrity.

AM: How do you spot an opportunity?

PN: Keep your antennae up.

AM: What would you have done differently if you could go back in time?

PN: Do it faster!

AM: How do you motivate yourself when things don't go to plan?

PN: Read a book. Listen to others. Listen to inspirational music.

MONEY AS A GOAL

Money is like food: the hungrier you get, the higher priority you give to eating. When you are completely full, you consider food a waste of time. Entrepreneurs should aim to be financially full, i.e. to have enough to live on for the foreseeable future.

For many people, entrepreneurship is about creativity and independence, and about working at what they want to do. They passionately love their work and would not change it to earn more money.

Other entrepreneurs focus on where the money is. They do what has to be done to maximize their financial status. Such people develop an incredible eye for profit and will certainly do whatever it takes.

Progress now

You have to identify your own values, drive and motivation.
What exactly is it about being an entrepreneur that appeals to
you?

List in order the top five things that interest you in being an
entrepreneur (e.g. financial freedom, wealth building,
creativity, control of your own destiny, independence,
developing your own ideas, inventing something, working from
home, retiring early).

1 _____

2 _____

3 _____

4 _____

5 _____

THREATS

Plan for dealing with failures right from the start. Thinking 'it will never happen to me' is just not smart.

Many entrepreneurs have a great deal of respect for their competitors and assume that around every corner they will be waiting in ambush. They are also self-critical, never satisfied with their own performance. Those that wallow in self-admiration are not focused on improving their efficiency and performance, believing they are already the best. This is the major difference between those that lead their industries and those that remain average. Do not take your client base for granted – customers can take a long time to develop yet will change loyalties in a second. Your competitors will probably ring them today with some new idea or promotions.

IF YOU COULD GO BACK FIVE YEARS

I have asked many of the entrepreneurs, 'If you could go back five years, what would you do differently?' They all learnt by their mistakes and kept trying and changing until things worked. Their most common wish was to have been more prudent with costs and better at communicating.

Many would-be entrepreneurs acquire initial funding then buy themselves flashy cars and all the trimmings. They are directors now and want the status of that success. They can finally pay themselves what they are worth. This does not communicate useful messages to staff, so they fail to win their real support. A true entrepreneur is a success when he or she runs a business at a profit, however small. Make financial and professional independence a higher priority than social status and focus on ideas that have a market you can reach. Start by redefining status as your opinion of yourself.

THE FIRST STEP IS THE HARDEST

If you have started your business and have made initial sales, however small, that is tremendous. You have proved there is a market for what you offer. You have changed from a theorist and dreamer to a realist.

Big mistake 1: A business is about making a better quality product at the best price

Wrong – a business is more about processes than it is about quality products. Customers are to a business what petrol is to a car: absolutely vital to go anywhere but there is a lot more to it than that. The car itself is a system of interacting parts working as a coordinated team in harmony. Similarly, if your business is an efficient machine it will operate at an optimum.

About five in every thousand business plans get funded. Those five will have received many rejections before being successful. One of the problems in the real world of starting a business is trying to eat and survive whilst you are designing the plan and presenting it to potential investors. You have to research and understand investment deals relative to the size you are seeking and the nature of your proposal.

GETTING STARTED

Services are an easier business to start than production businesses as you can begin small and build up. For example, if you are starting anything from a hairdresser to a management consultancy, all you need is your home telephone and a few pieces of equipment vital to your trade. A hairdresser will have the added advantage of immediate cash payments. If your idea is to develop a product, it may require all sorts of research, development, testing and patenting before purchasing capital equipment, stock and premises, and employing staff. Even then you can do a lot of this, without funding, in your evenings and weekends whilst maintaining a regular salary.

In summary, try to avoid raising money until you have developed as much as you can. The more you have proved your concept, the more likely you are to secure funding on good terms.

There are three categories of funding available to an entrepreneur: **loans**, **equity** and **wealth reservoir**.

LOANS

Loans are paid for with interest. You will find that loans for business purposes are not as easy to get as personal loans. A business carries an increased risk of default, so lenders are likely to demand some form of collateral to secure the loan if the business fails. Dreams, unfortunately, do not offer much by way of collateral. If the purpose of the loan is something tangible, such as vehicles, equipment or property, you will stand a better chance. If it is for 'fresh air investment' – advertising, marketing and research – it will be seen as more risky as the lender will have less to repossess.

If you have collateral to put up for a loan, do not assume that being made an offer is a vote of confidence in your business plan. It just means that it is not the lender's risk any more. Banks have a variety of loan philosophies. An old banking principle is match your collateral. Sometimes this is done with the support of a government scheme. Another principle is **balance sheet lending** – deciding the size of a loan according to the value of your balance sheet. Both philosophies can lead to bad loans and ignore in the viability of your business.

So look at your proposal from the point of view of the bank. How will your bank manager differentiate your proposal from hundreds of others? There is a naivety amongst would-be entrepreneurs that if they can persuade a bank manager of how good their idea is they will secure a loan. Taking risks is the speciality of another type of financial institution.

EQUITY: VENTURE CAPITAL EXPLAINED

Venture capitalists support businesses financially and in other ways , usually for a mixture of ordinary equity and loans. They are taking high risks in return for high potential payoffs. They will thus want to see considerable growth and an exit strategy, usually within three to five years.

Venture capitalists put in money in return for a share of the business. They can be broken down into two distinct groupings:

- **Wealthy individuals** who invest directly in companies. Typically this would be for amounts up to £250,000. At this level the enterprise is valued and they take a minority stake for their investment. They rarely want to control the enterprise although they certainly will want to keep in close touch with how their investment is doing. Many of these types of investor have business skills and contacts to offer as well.

  These people are sometimes called **business angels** and can often be identified through family or colleagues. Failing this, you can find them by attending specially organized events or using one of many business angel networks set up to make introductions. Business angels tend to invest in companies near to them or in an

CHAPTER 5: Going to plan?

119

industry that they know something about or have spotted as offering growth opportunities.

You can also find business angels through some firms of accountants or lawyers. They will often work on a contingency basis – no deal, no fee – and offer support services such as accounting and business plans. They also have a list of high net worth individuals as their clients. A potential investor is more likely to be impressed by a business plan that has been approved by a professional firm with a reputation at stake.

Institutional venture capitalists deal typically, though not necessarily, with larger amounts of money as part loan and part equity so that the management team can retain overall control.

As a general rule, the larger the amount, the easier it can be to raise, as the amount of work involved in assessing a proposal remains the same irrespective of the deal size. Venture capitalists cover their risk by the high potential payoffs of one of the ventures making it really big. They also syndicate their loans with other venturers. Different institutions tend to specialize in different amounts and different sectors of the economy. Again, you may do better by employing an intermediary: people in the investment business tend to have a strong preference to deal with someone they know. They also receive thousands of speculative business plans, so an established firm of accountants that they have done business with in the past is going to get far more attention.

An investor is buying the future value of your company. He or she will want a valuation according to your accounts and also an exit route to realize the investment. Then, of prime importance is the management team that will make the plan happen. Great ideas for businesses are ten a penny. Management teams that can make them happen are rare.

WEALTH RESERVOIR

This is one of the best funding routes. It is based on funding your business by using your creativity and ingenuity. It is the route that most successful firms take, with good reason:

- It gets you in to the habit of thrift and keeping overheads low — vital ingredients for success.

- Your time is spent developing the business.

- Pressure is on you to perform and this helps innovation.

- There is nobody on your back.

- There is no interest to pay or profits to share.

- You grow from the strong foundation of a proven market.

What is this wealth reservoir? It is the entrepreneurial mindset — using your brain and creativity to exploit resources that are already there but not fully utilized. This skill is not just used for product ideas. As soon as you can adopt this belief you will start to see a path forward. One of the faults of entrepreneurs is thinking that raising money ensures the success of their business. In practice it is just a start.

HOW TO MAKE YOUR OWN LUCK

Many people accuse successful entrepreneurs of being lucky. They are partly right, but those entrepreneurs took specific actions in order to get that luck. If someone wins the lottery by selecting a random group of numbers, this is pure luck; but when someone wins at cards, chess or backgammon, their luck has come from years of studying the game. Someone who wins great fortunes by investing in stocks and shares has done so by years of studying such investment. **Aristotle Onassis** was not lucky with his shipping investments: he religiously studied what was happening in his industry.

Whatever industry you are in, you must subscribe to the trade and professional press, set up a selective internet newsletter, attend forums and exhibitions, and keep informed. This way you will make knowledgeable decisions and significantly increase your fair share of luck. Energy exerted in business creates wealth. The more focused your energy, the more wealth you will create.

MARKETING YOUR WAY TO SALES

Marketing has been described as making the phone ring, and sales as closing a deal on answering it. **Sales** is about going out there with your product and making deals. It is therefore focused on your company's needs. **Marketing**, on the other hand, is putting resources into finding out and exploiting what consumers will pay. If your marketing is good, sales plays a far more minor role, so be a marketeer first and a salesperson second.

Entrepreneurs have a dream, and cannot wait to see it made real. They can be so caught up in their passion that they forget a basic principle of marketing: people pay money for what they want to buy, however irrational. Crazes in the toy market are created by the constant focus of entrepreneurs. Your idea could be the next craze.

To keep customers, ask — and keep asking — yourself down-to-earth questions:

- Are my customers satisfied?
- Have they been given a reason to be loyal to me?

- What can I do to improve my product?
- Are my new product ideas good in the customers' eyes?
- Is my idea as original as I think?
- Is it worth anything?
- Will it sell?
- Will it be copied or stolen by competitors?
- How do I reach the market?
- How much finance will I need to develop it?

MOVING ON

Many entrepreneurs start with just themselves and build from there. One of their common pitfalls is not replacing their instinctive decision making with processes. If you have a vision to be a big company one day, you must think of your company as a big one at its earliest stage.

The more people you employ, the more controls and decisions you will need to delegate. You therefore need to write a policy for every process so that things are controlled as you grow and new people need not reinvent any wheels. For example, you will need a policy on expenditure. As the owner of the business you will probably have been prudent, but employees may try to maximize the expenses they can get away with. Once you have a large organization it will be more difficult to change habits, so think ahead and make decisions now, not when the pressure is on. As soon as you establish an efficient way to do something, record it as policy. These documents must be accessible to your staff. This way no staff member can claim ignorance and the documents will save you a lot of management time.

THE CASE FOR PLANNING

Nobody plans to fail, but if you fail to plan you probably will. A **long-term focus** is essential for success. This includes considering every contingency and deciding what to do if it happens. It gives you direction and makes decision making easier along the way. The benefits of planning are perhaps best made through an analogy.

Two couples left for a month's sailing holiday. They filled the boat with provisions and decided to go where they pleased each day and not be tied down to a rigid timetable. Besides, it saved them a lot of boring planning and added some adventure.

- Was the holiday a success?
- How could you know? What criteria could you measure it against?
- Did everyone do what he or she individually wanted to do?
- Did the four people work as a team?
- Were their options restricted by not having the charts for certain waters?
- Did they find that something essential had not been packed?

🕭 Was provision made for mishap?

🕭 Were the costs divided equally and fairly?

🕭 Were they any arguments as to what to do and who would do what each day?

When the sea gets rough in the middle of the night is not the time to find out you do not have essential equipment and to decide whose shift it is. Yet this is exactly how many people manage their business and expect to be successful.

Progress now

Write a plan for your business that explains why and how it will work.

Chapter 6
Street strategies and tested techniques

Reading biographies does not mean try to be somebody else, but to be a better you through coaching from champions.

ALEX MCMILLAN

Like a boxer you have to be able to take the knocks and just fight on.

HOMAYOON FASSIHI

Progress now

Pick one of the following hot tips below and make it your focus for the week. Follow the advice given in this chapter. Then pick another, and so on.

1   Only buy at bargain prices.

2   Know the difference between an investment and a cost.

3   Turn your garage into an office.

4   Live within your means.

5   Cash is king.

6   Recruit the best and set them up to be outstanding.

7   Train an elite team.

8   Establish a corporate and team identity and culture.

9   Have a microscope and a telescope.

10 Catch the success virus.

11 Make negative words illegal.

12 Be decisive but explore all the options and implications first.

13 Be flexible – see from multiple perspectives.

14 Think ahead.

15	Play Monopoly.
16	Always have a plan B.
17	Harness your whole concentration upon one goal.
18	Provide what people want to buy.
19	Get free publicity and advertising.
20	Spread the word.
21	If in doubt, raise prices.
22	Right place, right time.
23	Think opportunity.
24	Ask a lot of 'why' questions.
25	Move fast.
26	Keep it simple.
27	Do what has to be done.
28	Keep to your strength areas – you have advantages here.

28 STRATEGIES

1 Only buy at bargain prices

If it is not a bargain, haggle, shop around, do without, take other routes, wait until it is a bargain. In negotiation, time and waiting are a powerful influencing tool, so never be in a hurry when buying. Refer to the life stories of **Paul Getty** and **Warren Buffet** and see how these billionaires have mastered this principle.

2 Know the difference between an investment and a cost

Poorly performing entrepreneurs do not understand the difference between a cost and an investment. Investments are things that you want more of, because they make an eventual and regular contribution to profit. Costs, on the other hand, reduce profit and need keeping to a minimum without adversely affecting operations. Look at your own business and differentiate costs from investments in the last month.

3 Turn your garage into an office

Running a business profitably is all about keeping costs down. At the end of the day, business runs to the equation Sales − Costs = Profits.

The wise also realize that there is a difference between good and bad costs. A good cost is one that directly increases sales or the potential for sales. Any other cost is something that threatens you. At some point in a business life cycle, cash inflows will go down for whatever reason. If your minimum cost base is less than that of your competitors you will probably outlast them. The more cost you amass, the quicker you will be threatened.

In the 1980s in Britain there was a household name airline called Air Europe. Since inception, its report and accounts showed a significant growth in both sales and profits for every year. Then the Gulf War happened; Air Europe went bust and its office contents were auctioned. The luxurious furniture and thick carpets went for less than a tenth of their original price. Air Europe's nest-egg against a turndown was wasteful and needless luxuries.

Buy your computers, carpets and furniture secondhand or cheaply. Mind the pennies, and the pounds will look after themselves.

4 Live within your means

Many people earning a high income still manage to get into debt. The big spenders are not the rich: they know how to keep hold of their money and not be tempted against their best interests. Big spenders tend to be people using credit to bolster their self-esteem.

5 Cash is king

When it comes to accounting, entrepreneurs seem to focus on cash flow. They see their business in simple terms, even when it becomes larger. They concentrate on increasing cash in and reducing cash out. When it comes to the balance sheet they think of assets as things that produce income and of liabilities as things that cost them money. Accountants see property, fixtures and fittings and motor vehicles as assets. As these things cost money to run, entrepreneurs see them as liabilities. Key people are not usually valued in the accounts. The **Virgin Group's** accounts will show Richard Branson's PC as an asset, but not him. Personally, if I had Richard Branson advising my enterprises I would consider that a very valuable asset that I would use to the full.

6 Recruit the best and set them up to be outstanding

The first rule is to make it difficult to get a job with your company, through a rigorous recruitment process. The second rule is don't try to get the best staff by relying on paying the highest salaries. People naturally value things according to how much effort it takes to achieve them. Think of the organizations that you consider to be leading in their field and then look at how they recruit.

How do you create a tough recruitment process? There are various methods: many interviews, panel interviews, aptitude and personality tests and assessment days. The best way is to use an outside agency to do the shortlist assessments. This sends a message to would-be applicants as to just how seriously you take your recruitment process. It raises the value of a job with you in their eyes. Identify the exact profile of who you wish to recruit and keep looking until you have found them.

Bill Gates went to great lengths to recruit the best quality staff. He even bought whole companies when he could not headhunt their key staff directly.

7 Train an elite team

Training is often something that is considered important but not urgent and thus keeps getting postponed. Training, when picked carefully, is not a cost but an investment with a long-term return. It gives you an edge over your competition. It can make you more efficient in any of the functions of your business. It is also motivational to staff.

Training return is limited by the quality of the staff being trained. You should initially spend time clarifying your recruitment policy and processes. Recruit the best and you will also get the bonus of a better return from the training you give them.

Training should be for you as well as your staff. **Paul Getty** learnt foreign languages to help in his business dealings.

8 Establish a corporate and team identity and culture

Another book in this series offers some great ideas about teams. Entrepreneurial companies that really go places identify a strong team and corporate culture early on then recruit people whose personalities match that culture and identity. This they put before job competences, as skills training will be a lot easier than personality changing. If a person really fits in with the team, they can usually be trained in any skills they lack.

Progress now

Think of the five companies that you admire the most for whatever reason. They may be of any size or industry.

1 _____
2 _____
3 _____
4 _____
5 _____

Now write down the five things that you admire the most about these companies.

What policies and ideas can you apply to your enterprise from this list?

SIMON MCBETH

Simon founded and now manages CC Associates Ltd and is leading the merger of several professional services companies, including his own, into a group which he heads. His aim is to become a major name by offering a quality of service and way of operating that is quite different from the current industry set-up.

AM: What is your career background?

SM: It was on a six-month holiday scuba diving in Barbados with time to think that I realized that my long-term ambition was to run and grow my own business. I was 24 years old and knew that I wanted to make a lot of money building a business. My passion was so great I knew that nothing would stop me until I had achieved it. I want to be in charge of my own destiny and believe that anyone can be a successful entrepreneur.

My first objective was to save up some money. I worked for a lottery company and was given the challenge for setting up a call centre for 140 staff in a totally empty building. I achieved this ahead of schedule. I then went on to set up call centres for other major companies. A soon as I had completed them I rapidly became bored.

I set up CC Associates in 1999 and established a reputation for delivering what I promised within deadlines. In fact I was soon regularly turning work away. I worked from home, albeit mostly out with clients, building the business. I have always believed in no frills unless absolutely necessary. I am in some ways unusual because I do not tell customers what I think they want to hear, but instead tell them the reality. I then always deliver what I say I will.

I kept hearing from companies that were dissatisfied with the service they received from others. I encouraged them to talk and listened to them, rather than focusing on what we could offer – an approach that differentiated us. I ask a lot of questions and believe that there is no such thing as a stupid question.

Having made a commitment, my approach is to get going, learn by mistakes fast and always deliver whatever it takes. I focus on people, processes and profitability.

AM: How do you define success?

SM: Being happy in what you do.

AM: What is the secret of success of an entrepreneur?

SM: Even if you have to make 56 attempts it will happen if you don't give up. Nobody has ever succeeded as an entrepreneur without making many mistakes. You need to be very single-minded.

AM: What advice would you give somebody starting out?

SM: 1 Be clear about what you want to do.

2 Success has to be earned.

3 Be thick skinned.

4 Don't take anything personally.

5 Keep going.

6 Earn your luck by fighting for it.

AM: How do you spot opportunities?

SM: Be out there looking for them constantly. Being an entrepreneur is like being a policeman – you are never off duty.

AM: What would you have done differently if you could go back in time?

SM: Researched the market better and developed the business quicker.

AM: How do you motivate yourself when things don't go to plan?

SM: I strongly believe in myself and learn from my mistakes.

9 Have a microscope and a telescope

Focus on what is immediately in front of you **and** on the horizon. An interesting pattern among entrepreneurs is that they tend to talk about what they are going to do rather than what they have achieved. Their focus is the future – they look for opportunities, don't get bogged down in old ways of doing things and stay positive when experiencing failures.

The entrepreneur that really steams ahead is the one that can learn from the past and also see good in the future – the person who is very flexible and takes many different perspectives before coming to decisions. The long-term strategist and visionary is blended with the practical, active person.

10 Catch the success virus

Would you bet £1000 on a roulette wheel to win £1 million if 22 came up or lose everything otherwise?

Would you gamble £10,000 on anything other than 22 coming up if you stood to win £1 million?

If you stood to win £10 million if anything but 22 came up, but would be shot if 22 came up, would you take the bet?

(141)

What would a self-made millionaire do? They would find another game where they could determine the stakes, the odds and have a strong influence on the outcome. Entrepreneurs don't play roulette – they have no time for games of chance. Entrepreneurs design their own game, reduce the odds of losing, increase the odds of winning and cover for the downside.

11 Make negative words illegal

Words that you hear generate internal pictures and determine your feelings.

- Cover your workplace walls with positive pictures, suggestions, quotes and words.

- Open a negative word box. Every time someone makes a negative statement they have to put money into the box then rephrase what they have said in a positive way.

12 Be decisive but explore all the options and implications first

You must learn how to wait and be patient. Ascertain anything that could go wrong and base your decisions on as much information as you can. Take as much time as you need to make those decisions.

13 Be flexible – see from multiple perspectives

Keep trying different approaches until you are successful. Looking at a challenge from a different point of view often produces ideas. Ask other people their opinion. Look at everything first from the customer's point of view.

14 Think ahead

Always think about anything that could go wrong in the future. This is deliberately making yourself think negatively. Now you have time on your side to work out what to do. You can even take it a step further and figure out how you could benefit from the event transpiring. Everything that happens in business has a positive side and the easiest way to exploit it is to think ahead of time.

15 Play Monopoly

The young **Bill Gates** was an avid player of Monopoly. You can learn and apply a lot of its principles. For example, certain players will always go for the expensive streets, but these people very rarely win.

More often than not, the winner is the person that buys the mid-range streets, with a good balance of investment to return. The cheapest streets are handy to generate cash flow but take for ever to generate a reasonable sum of wealth. The stations offer four places with a reasonably frequent return without any building costs. You will never win on this set but they can finance you as you go along, keeping the cash flowing.

Chance and Community Chest are realistic to life. The wise player knows all the cards that can come up and sets something aside for the worst scenario. The best way to learn from Monopoly is to play with friends for real money. That way the lessons will be logged into your unconscious as you are getting real business experience.

16 Always have a plan B

One of the traits common to all successful entrepreneurs is that they think ahead and consider every scenario. **Aristotle Onassis**, **John D. Rockefeller** and **Paul Getty**'s biographies clearly show this trait again and again. So often when their opponents thought they had caught them out they would show that they had made contingency plans for exactly that situation. In your business, ask yourself what could go wrong in the next three months. What can you do now to prepare for it, or even to create opportunities from it?

17 Harness your whole concentration upon one goal

If you have five things to achieve, the more sequentially you can do them the more success you will have. Attending to five things at once usually means that none of them is achieved. If you focus your mind on one goal, your thinking will be much clearer and produce better answers.

18 Provide what people want to buy

Entrepreneurs have a real passion for their ideas and products. This does not mean that the buying public will. What people want or should want can be very different from what they will part with money for. The best products are those that were initiated by seeing a need in the market and then supplying it, not the other way around.

19 Get free publicity and advertising

Before you spend a small fortune on promoting your business, seek out and exploit all the free ways first. You can write articles for online and print periodicals, do radio or TV interviews or give free seminars. Try at least five ways of getting free coverage before you spend anything on advertising.

20 Spread the word

The most effective, most reliable and cheapest marketing is word of mouth and personal recommendation. People who are buying on recommendation are also less likely to haggle on price as they are already convinced of quality and service.

21 If in doubt, raise prices

There are three reasons why, if you are in doubt, you should raise your prices:

1   Most people associate price with quality.
2   Higher prices will generate profit even if volume drops.
3   Volume may go up.

22 Right place, right time

There are golden rules of entrepreneurship that allow an enterprise to be launched and developed from the first stages to profit. The really big stars seem to have an additional ability of being in the right place at the right time.

To be in the right place at the right time as a business entrepreneur is not to invent your goods then take them to market but to do it the other way around: find out what people need then go away and invent it.

Progress now

What three major changes have happened around you in the last year?

1 _____

2 _____

3 _____

What new needs do they create?

1 _____

2 _____

3 _____

Which of these are you in a position to exploit?

_____

_____

_____

23 Think opportunity

Always be looking for opportunity. For example, when negotiating with a supplier, can you put any other business their way? How about more favourable terms in return for your displaying their brochures in your office or a link on your website?

24 Ask a lot of 'why' questions

'Why' questions get you in the habit of challenging the status quo, and thus of identifying even more opportunities.

25 Move fast

Business is about deadlines, and meeting them is an essential step to success. Put deadlines before quality. Get something to market fast then continually improve it. If you wait for perfection, the market will have moved on. **Microsoft**® has spent years developing and improving an operating system for common use. Its earlier versions were riddled with bugs and breakdowns but it still offered more than its competitors. Customer feedback then led to enhancements.

26 Keep it simple

A very well-worn business principle, but one followed by all that are successful. Business is not an intellectual exercise – don't try to turn it into one.

27 Do what has to be done

As your own boss you are free to decide what to do each day. Most of us naturally will focus on what we want to do. Instead, ask yourself what needs to be done as a priority in order to meet your goals, then concentrate on achieving it.

28 Keep to your strengths – you have advantages here

Know your strengths and keep to them. Delegate everything else as soon as possible. Your time is precious and in short supply so maintain its usefulness at maximum output. Doing the accounts yourself, for example, is not a thrifty habit but a lavish one. What will take you a week and not be done properly can be done in two hours by a professional accountant.

Progress now

Forget answers and think of questions. Design ten questions, however unreasonable and unrealistic, for which you would like answers.

1 _____

2 _____

3 _____

4 _____

5 _____

6 _____

7 _____

8 _____

9 _____

10 _____

Chapter 7

How Better Knowledge Can Make You a Better Entrepreneur

The secret of business is to know something that nobody else knows.

ARISTOTLE ONASSIS

Trust your own judgement and never be afraid to change.

RICHARD BAXTER

QUALITY ADVICE THAT IS VALUE FOR MONEY

Be wary of 'expert' advice. People have a great tendency to answer any question you ask them. Hardly anyone will admit 'I don't know the answer to that one.'

When you need guidance, seek it from at least three independent experts and be careful not to let them know either your opinion or that you have talked to other experts. Advice that confers from all three has a high chance of being good advice.

Experts charge high rates for their advice, good or bad. There are, however, various ways to get free advice. The first and easiest of these is the internet. You can surf a whole range of information and check it with other sources. You can e-mail experts from their websites and put your questions to them. Invariably they will answer your question in the hope of winning your respect and making you a client.

There are also governmental organizations, central and local, which give citizens free advice. Banks have a range of information on specific challenges relating to entrepreneurial businesses that they will give you free of charge. There are also many professional and trade associations that provide free services to members.

Only take advice from someone who has practical experience in what you are enquiring about. Do not take advice from someone who has a vested interest unless that interest is totally in line with your own. Potential suppliers of services are looking to make sales. Their job is to sell to you and argue in favour of what they offer.

WHAT KNOWLEDGE DO YOU REQUIRE TO BE A SUCCESSFUL ENTREPRENEUR?

You need knowledge of:

- How to write a business plan
- Your industry
- Your market
- Processes
- Competitors
- What could go wrong
- The outlook for the future
- How to raise money
- Pricing strategy

The list is endless, so knowing where to find answers quickly and cheaply for your business is essential. Your decisions are limited by the knowledge you have. You have to learn to use those people and resources around you that already have that knowledge. Remember: knowledge only becomes power when acted upon.

KNOWLEDGE OF THE LAW

Bill Gates, **Richard Branson** and **Howard Hughes** all had lawyers in their family. To be an entrepreneur you need a streetwise knowledge of the law — a practical understanding of what should happen if someone does not pay you or breaks a contract. What, in reality, can you do about it? The law may be on your side, but getting paid is a different matter. Chasing money through the courts can take months or years.

Be mean with your signature and always read small print: it can come back to haunt you. Don't be afraid to renegotiate a standard contract or take your business elsewhere. Be aware of any statutes that will apply irrespective of anything agreed in a contract. In any complex matter use an accountant or solicitor.

KNOWLEDGE OF MONEY

All you need to know about money is your bank balance and how much money is going out and in over the coming weeks. Everything else should be delegated to experts.

Entrepreneurs don't suffer vanity. The ones that really make it big keep their expenditure to a survival minimum until their business is established. Part of being thrifty is knowing where you are financially at any point.

KNOWLEDGE OF THE DIFFERENCE BETWEEN AN ASSET AND A LIABILITY

Entrepreneurs think in very simple terms. An **asset** is something that **increases** your wealth, a **liability** something that **reduces** your wealth. The object of business is to increase assets relative to liabilities. Look at every aspect of your business and establish whether it is an asset or a liability. What can you do to increase the wealth-earning properties of your assets. What can you do to reduce the wealth-draining properties of your liabilities?

Take an audit as follows:

1 What assets do you have and how much do they make for you?

   a) How could they make you more money?

   b) What can you do to acquire more assets?

   c) What around you could become an asset?

2 What liabilities do you have and how much do they cost you?

   a) How could they be reduced?

   b) How could they be eliminated?

Some items have an element of both asset and liability. For example, a sales representative costing £70,000 pa in salary and related costs brings in sales of £150,000 pa. He or she is an asset worth £80,000. On the other hand, a bookkeeper costing £30,000 pa in salary and related costs is a liability as he or she does not bring in sales so you should monitor productivity relative to cost.

Progress now

Are the following assets, liabilities or both?

Property _____

Cars _____

Computers _____

Stationery _____

Shares _____

Royalties _____

It is interesting to note that entrepreneurs think about money quite differently from their corporate counterparts. Assets to accountants and bankers are things they can repossess: property, fixtures and fittings, goodwill, money owed, computers, other equipment. Do these things make money or cost money to run?

WHAT ARE YOUR ASSETS?

To audit your business you need to put a capital value on each asset. To a recruitment agency, for example, an introduction fee would be about £3000 for an average employee. Therefore each of your staff needs to be valued at this figure. Your contacts and customers can all be assets in this way if they are potential sources of income.

People that can be defined as liabilities are usually quite necessary to the business. Therefore, the gains to be made are not just on reducing their costs but also in making them more efficient. What is the value they are adding to the organization? Can this be done more cheaply, or can they be made more productive for the same money?

Progress now

Complete the following asset audit for your business. A few examples have been included.

Item	Estimated value	Possible value	Action
ASSETS			
KEY PEOPLE			
You	£100,000	£200,000	Improve time management
Harry, sales manager	£75,000	£100,000	Training course
Mary, telesales	£35,000	£75,000	Manage and motivate
Products	£35,000	£50,000	Change marketing strategy
Ideas			
Contacts			
Database			
LIABILITIES			
Rent			
Salaries			
Stationery			
Advertising			

KEEPING YOUR FINGER ON THE PULSE

Many entrepreneurs are so caught up in day-to-day challenges that they have no time to sit down and think. If they did so, they would predict many of the events that eventually become news.

Once you start becoming a leader and making the news, you have started to control your destiny. Like the surfer riding waves, you have to harness the energy of what is there, predict what is coming and react quickly. An unforeseen wave is what will knock you down – not the wave itself but the fact that you did not see it coming.

Make sure that you invest time to keep well informed of whatever industry you are in. Keep asking yourself **ODQs – opportunity directional questions**:

- Where is this all leading?
- How does this affect me?
- How could I benefit from this?
- What does not exist now but there is clearly an emerging demand for?
- What opportunities are advances in technology releasing?
- If I had £1 million to invest right now, what would I do with it?

Progress now

1 Think of something that you may find on the beach.

2 Apply any ideas, shapes, textures and thoughts associated to that item to the idea of opening a restaurant.

3 Consider the raw idea generated above and make it more commercially viable.

For example, your might think of sand then imagine having an egg timer on each table. When customers sit down they turn the egg timer over. The restaurant promises to serve the customer before the egg timer is empty or they get a free bottle of wine.

Commercial advantages:

1 No real cost

2 Advertising theme on promising to be served in less time than it takes to boil an egg

3 Novelty and a fun atmosphere created in the restaurant

4 People come for the chance to get free wine

5 Free publicity in local papers and other media

6 Logo and address on printed egg cups which people can take with them and use when booking a table

WHERE THE IDEAS COME FROM

The Progress now box on the previous page illustrates that inspiration for ideas often comes while away from work because of your different frame of mind.

Your initial ideas will be crude and need refining but they will give you the jump-start you need.

INTERVIEW

HOMAYOON FASSIHI

Homayoon is managing director of DMN Nursing Agency which has clients all over London and East Anglia.

AM: What is your career background?

HM: I always wanted my own business and was constantly seeing opportunities everywhere I looked. I believe that being an entrepreneur is something that is just in me. I have that type of personality where I want to reap a higher level of reward but am realistically prepared to be punished harshly if it goes wrong.

I noticed at a hairdresser that the manager was sending a staff member to the local launderette with a fistful of money for the machine. This to me seemed inefficient. I asked the manager how much it cost him to have all his towels washed. He added up the machine cost and the staff member's wages for the time they were away from the salon. I said, 'If there was a service that could pick up, clean and deliver back your towels, at a lower price, would you be interested?' He said yes, of course. I said, 'I'll be back.'

My idea was that if I had such a contract with all the local hairdressers, collection and delivery would be cost effective. I also realized that the marginal cost of running a washing machine was next to nothing.

In the end I bought a launderette. I largely ignored the walk-in business. By the end of the year the launderette's turnover, let alone profit, was five times larger than when I had bought it. I literally knocked on doors and gained as many contracts as I could. Hairdressers were an obvious client. Business was booming and there was a need for a dry cleaning service, so I bought a retail dry cleaners on a prime site with a view to using all of its spare capacity.

In year two I brought in new contracts which included a major London hairdressing chain, two airlines, a local theatre and TV company, two Royal Air Force camps, five big hotels and a suit hire shop. The machines were literally working around the clock I was working 18-hour days.

I then sold the launderette together with all the contracts. I later did the same thing with the dry cleaners. During that time there were many challenges on many fronts. I also had many other unsuccessful ventures along the way.

My next big idea was of a niche nursing agency offering a certain type of service. I set up from scratch and now run this business having personally brought in £1 million worth of clients. I am also currently developing a business plan for a programme of personal security courses and a web portal focused on Ireland.

I have been to banks to support me and have been rejected many times, but now with a track record of success I find that the bank comes to me. If you have proved you can make money, everybody will look at your ideas. The first real success is the hardest but you have to keep working at it. Having had my fingers burnt has taught me to always be cautious with money. I believe that it is relatively easy to win new business – you need to put far more emphasis on keeping it.

AM: How do you define success?

HF: Knowing you have created something good and added value from your ideas. It is a feeling of self-confidence, shown by the way you walk and hold your head. Sometimes it is measured in the way other people respond to you.

AM: What is the secret of success of an entrepreneur?

HF: Think and plan long term and work 18 hours per day on what needs doing now. The payoff comes in, say, two years' time, so focus on this.

AM: What advice would you give somebody starting out?

HF: 1 Work hard.

2 Don't give up.

3 Be enthusiastic.

4 Be stubborn.

5 Be honest. People will always accept a shortfall if you are honest and explain.

6 Never blame others – take responsibility for everything.

AM: How do you spot an opportunity?

HF: I just feel that something is right, and this in itself generates an enthusiasm. Even if it does not work out, it becomes invaluable experience for the future.

AM: What would you have done differently if you could go back in time?

HF: I would be more careful about picking who I work with. I would learn how to say no.

AM: How do you motivate yourself when things don't go to plan?

HF: Like a boxer, you have to be able to take the knocks and just fight on.

KNOW YOUR ADVANTAGES

Traditional economists like to talk of economies of scale bringing advantages as companies become larger. Less seems to have been written on what could be called 'acorn advantages' — the advantages of being a small growth company. Consider the following:

Growth company	*Large company*
Simple management structure	Complex management
All managers deal direct with customers	Few managers deal with customers
Personal service	Bureaucracy
Call any time	Voicemail jail, rarely get through
All staff produce or sell	Many administrative functions
Quick decisions	Slow decisions
Lead from the front	Head office decisions get passed down

Whatever your industry, there will be both economies of scale and acorn advantages. It is important that you can recognize both in order to help your decision making. In fact, so important have acorn advantages become that many large companies have gone to great lengths to build autonomous small companies with minimal head office functions to maintain the energy and advantage of being small.

Of course, you can use franchising or network marketing and gain the advantages of being big and small, as **McDonald's** and **Amway** have done, both producing a substantial number of very wealthy people.

Progress now

Think of a small business near you. What three advantages of being small are they failing to exploit?

Chapter 8
Better Skills Than Your Competitors

There is no such thing as a stupid question.

SIMON MCBETH

Don't borrow: buy what you want, when you can afford it.

AUSTIN REYNOLDS

SKILLS FROM OTHER ASPECTS OF YOUR LIFE

Sensei Paul Elliott has built up a thriving karate school and develops in his students many valuable skills which are useful in many ways. He has coached many adults and children to black belt level and has built a business that is his passion. He is living his dream.

In life and in business, Paul says you should know how to:

- Be totally sensitive to what is going on around you
- Conquer ego and vanity
- Be disciplined
- Be respectful
- Be humble
- Be well behaved
- Take a fall without being hurt
- Fight whilst being on the ground
- Keep fighting after several blows
- Fight against someone of higher skill or advantage

- ۵ Change your style
- ۵ Never give up
- ۵ Keep fighting fit
- ۵ Avoid fights

Not surprisingly, many of Paul's students are successful entrepreneurs.

SKILLS AT MANAGING TIME

Who hasn't had an opportunity come their way and talked and thought about it until the opportunity has gone? That is the problem with opportunities: they tend to have a short shelf-life. You need to analyse and make full and proper judgements but must recognize when the time for action has arrived. Work on refining your judgement skills so as to make an effective balance between not being too hasty and hesitating.

SKILLS AT GETTING THE BEST OUT OF EVERYTHING

You have £10,000 to invest so you go to five well-established banks.

- ◐ The first one offers you 10 per cent interest.
- ◐ The second offers 8 per cent interest.
- ◐ The third offers 4 per cent interest.
- ◐ The fourth offers no interest at all.
- ◐ The fifth would charge you 10 per cent interest to look after your money.

How would you spread your investment amongst the banks?

I would put it all in the one paying 10 per cent and look forward in year two to having 10 per cent on the first year interest as well. You would probably do the same. If you were extremely risk averse and not trusting of banks you might spread it equally amongst the first four to reduce the possible downside. Anyone would be mad to make a deposit in bank 5.

In your business you have a whole range of resources: money, contacts, goodwill, client databases, computers, web pages, people, premises, cars, ideas, market intelligence, locations etc. What rate of return are you getting from these resources?

Progress now

1   Write a list of all the resources of any nature you currently have in your business.

_____

_____

_____

2   Assess, as a percentage, whether you are getting a full return, part return, zero return or negative return from each resource.

3   Decide what you can do to maximize the return from each resource.

4   Repeat this exercise every month, ensuring that the returns from each resource are included in your new resource list.

5   Now take a moment to think of the three resources you have at your disposal but have omitted from the list above.

_____

_____

_____

SKILLS OF DEVELOPING GOOD HABITS

There are two aspects to developing good habits: breaking redundant or destructive habits and forming new, useful ones. Forming new ones is easier. The beauty of habits is that once they are formed they happen without any conscious effort.

Progress now

Type on your PC and print out the following in an attractive colour, print size and type.

Success Focus

Five things that are really good news at the moment:

1 _____
2 _____
3 _____
4 _____
5 _____

My three targets for this week:

1 _____

2 _____

3 _____

One thing I will give myself as a reward for accomplishing the above:

_____

Attach a blank copy to the wall at the start of each week. Fill in the answers and refer to them briefly each day. This simple exercise will help you to maintain a consistently positive outlook.

SKILLS WITH INFORMATION MANAGEMENT

Established businesses have a great deal of information at their disposal: statistics on their business, client databases, all their experience and lessons so far. Entrepreneurs face uncertainty, with no track record and limited resources. New products or ideas do not have trends that can be analysed so easily. For this they need to be in touch with their potential market. The internet has changed this dramatically, allowing free access to near-infinite research material.

SKILLS AT MANAGING CAPITAL

Only risk getting into debt if the capital being invested is expected to earn a better rate of return than you are paying. That is how you can make money. Never spend a penny on anything that is not mission critical whilst you are in debt. Every penny saved is a penny invested in your business.

Prepare for every eventuality you can think of. However well you do this you will still find yourself facing something completely unexpected. The way to deal with this is to have some reserve ready to tide you over a lean period.

SKILLS AT MANAGING EXPENSES

Expenses have a habit of rising up to meet your sales income. Too many companies only investigate and monitor costs when a cool wind blows. Cost discipline is more important during the good times when the pressure is off and it is no longer your main focus. Entrepreneurs make the mistake of getting carried away with their own success – a recipe for future failure.

When negotiating contracts, inspect terms, propose changes and shop around until you find someone that will deal on your terms. Be stubborn and persistent and you will prevail. To be an entrepreneur you have to fight your corner and fight for every penny.

The most effective action is to inspire cost-saving behaviour. These examples come from interviews with successful entrepreneurs:

- ℧ Instead of a serviced office, convert your garage.
- ℧ Buy laptops and PCs at auctions.
- ℧ Travel economy class.
- ℧ Use the phone to communicate if travel can be avoided.

- Send an e-mail rather than make a telephone call.
- Incentivize staff with bonuses linked to results.
- Avoid mobile phones unless absolutely essential.
- Use e-mail instead of paper post.
- Utilize all the free advertising and promotional methods available to you before spending.
- Drive used cars or use public transport.
- Buy your office furniture secondhand.
- Whenever possible, have staff based at home.
- Know about and take any government assistance available.
- Focus on one thing at a time, get that up and running then focus on the next thing.

SKILLS AT STANDING APART

A trait of the self-made rich is that they tend to move in the opposite direction to most investors. **Paul Getty** was a classic example of this. Throughout his business career he constantly went against the crowd. He bought in a down market, sold in a booming market, invested in countries that his competitors were pulling out of and expanded during recessions.

USING YOUR SKILLS TO BE FREE

Money, to a lot of people, means fear of the lack of it. Wanting to be financially free is a good goal for an entrepreneur, even if that is not the main goal. Your main motivation to make money should be really loving what you do, which usually means controlling your own destiny and amassing money as a pleasant side-effect.

DOES MCDONALD'S HAVE THE BEST SKILLS IN GRILLING THE BEST BURGERS?

Entrepreneurs see a business as a machine to make money. If the machine works well they then duplicate it and make more money. Entrepreneurs focus far less on that magical product that will catch the public imagination and sell like hot cakes. Think of your business enterprise as designing a system to make money. Many inventors and entrepreneurs go wrong because they think success is all about coming up with a winning product.

McDonald's entrepreneur **Ray Kroc** bought the original restaurant from the two McDonald brothers and was obsessed with details and processes. He listed every process in the operation until it was as efficient as possible. He designed a business system. When it was finished he duplicated profit by duplicating the winning formula. His target was to own as much property as possible – he was not interested in burgers.

Richard Branson is one of the world's most successful record producers. Was he a music lover, a musician who wanted to run his own label? No. He was in touch with what musicians could offer and what teenagers wanted to buy, and matched the two in a business system called Virgin Records.

Too much interest in the product can take your focus off the business. If your priority is profits, your focus must be on producing your goods and getting them to market in an efficient manner.

SKILLS AT READING PEOPLE

A common mistake for someone new in the entrepreneur business is assuming that people are logical and rational and will make buying decisions according to their best interests. It does not work that way.

Progress now

Go to your local supermarket and watch the shoppers as they make decisions to buy things. Look specifically at how they walk, stop, plan their route through the shop, backtrack, pause, are influenced by merchandising or not, talk to other shoppers, talk to staff, put things back, put things in their trolley and look at prices.

- What different patterns do you notice emerging?
- Are there any differences according to socio-economic groupings?
- Are there clear stereotypes evident?
- How logical and rational do you think people are when making buying decisions?

Progress now

Does anything frustrate you?

_____

_____

Is there an aspect of the world around you that could be better?

_____

_____

What would you like to see done about it?

_____

_____

How could you do something about it at a profit?

_____

_____

Every aspect of every enterprise can be improved then improved again. That is a belief worth adopting because it will make you look constantly for improvement. Even after you have just improved a system, you must immediately start criticizing to find the next level of improvement. Start by looking at a market and seeing how the current suppliers operate. If you can spot a need for improvement, you have an opportunity. Entrepreneurs don't just create new products and services: they look to produce the same things at a lower unit cost.

Look for waste – in time, materials, finance, energy, manpower and market advantages. As organizations grow, they tend to develop surpluses. These are usually things that were once useful but no longer serve a purpose such as reports that nobody reads.

SKILLS AT TIME MANAGEMENT

The most efficient skill of an entrepreneur is managing your time effectively, as shown in the example opposite.

Progress now

Replace the list in the example with tasks that you do in a typical week. Put them in order of importance. Note in your diary how much time you spend on each and total it up for the week. Now set a target to eradicate, delegate and reduce time spent on the items lower down the list and to spend that time on items higher up the list.

Mary Jones runs her own business. Her added value to the business is estimated at £20,000 per month so each hour of her time is worth £100. The value of each hour's work depends upon the level at which she is working. If she always tries to work at a higher pay rate, she will add more value to her enterprise.

1	Taking action to make deals	£500 ph
2	Creating and developing	£400 ph
3	On the telephone	£100 ph
4	Meeting people	£100 ph
5	Training new staff	£75 ph
6	E-mailing	£50 ph
7	Meeting sales representatives	£25 ph
8	Surfing the computer for information	£10 ph
9	Filing	£5 ph
10	Looking for lost papers	£1 ph
11	Waiting to be connected	£1 ph

Time management has particular relevance to entrepreneurs because when they start they will usually be alone or certainly in a small group and therefore responsible for all aspects of the company. Changing hats between accountant, salesperson, recruiter and creator is going to make challenging demands on your time. When you grow bigger, labour will become more specialized and thus more efficient.

This means that you have to be very disciplined. You have to distil your long-term vision to a quarterly, monthly, weekly then daily objective list. This way you know that at the end of every day you have moved that much closer to your goal. This is the simplest and most effective way to make sure that you are productive and not just busy.

SKILLS AT DRAWING OUT GOOD IDEAS FROM THE PEOPLE AROUND YOU

Progress now

Next week do something different – anything at all, even as small as wearing your watch on the other wrist or dressing differently. You will be pleasantly surprised how breaking one minor habit gives you the advantage of a new perspective and the ability to break bigger habits.

When you are starting to think and plan, ignore such boring concepts as possibility. When a telesales person was asked what she would like if she could have any product at all, however unreasonable, she answered:

'I would like a phone system that had a screen with four sections on it. The display would have on it in real time what the other person was saying, top left, and thinking, bottom left. In addition it would show suggested answers to their questions, top right, and suggested questions to ask, bottom right.'

Now if you could make such a product there is clearly a market for it. With the accurate digital electronics and sophisticated software available it is possible to go a long way towards exactly that. Subtle changes in voice tone could be identified and meanings printed on screen. Verbal and non-verbal voice patterns could be analysed in real time.

Progress now

Ask five people around you: 'If you could buy any product at all that does not even exist yet, what would you buy? Be as unreasonable as you like.'

People will respond with all sorts of weird ideas. This is the raw material which you can then sculpt into a workable commercial prospect.

SKILLS AT CHOOSING THE RIGHT PEOPLE

Staff can be your greatest but also your highest-risk asset. They can perform badly, be ill, need constant supervision, have emotional problems, let you down, arrive late, resign, sell your secrets to competitors or go on strike. At the end of each month, though, there is one certainty: they will want their cheques. If you have had half the sales that month they are unlikely to be happy with half salaries.

When employing staff, think very carefully before making an offer. At interview both you and the interviewee are likely to create expectations you cannot fulfil. Nearly every manager has had experiences of people not turning out as expected from the interview. Nearly every employee has a story of broken promises.

SKILLS AT COLD CALLING

When starting a new venture, you will have to attract customers from a cold start. For almost all professional salespeople, cold calling is the activity they dread most. Part of this is the balance in their mind of success to failure. They can make 100 calls before they make a sale. So their mind is registering that 99 per cent of their time is unproductive, producing a growing feeling of rejection and failure.

Use this simple equation to change your perception:

How many appointments turn into a deal?	X
How much is the value of the average deal?	Y
How many calls on average does it take to get an appointment?	Z

Then each call is worth Z multiplied by Y divided by X

For example, if your average deal size is £6000 (Y), one in three visits (X) is turned into a deal and it takes on average 100 calls (Z) to make an appointment, then the value of each call is £20. If you get your sales team to focus on this figure, they will concentrate on making more than £20 and will therefore make more calls. If, on the other hand, they make 90 calls and feel they have achieved nothing, their motivation level will drop significantly.

Sell to people who are prospects for what you have to sell. It is always easier to sell to people who have already bought a similar product. A new book is sold to people who have bought books before. A new style of trainer will appeal to people who have previously bought trainers. It sounds obvious, but millions are spent daily by entrepreneurs relearning these lessons the hard way.

SKILLS AT SELLING

Many people have a fear of selling, and many of those people are in selling! This fear can be overcome in a few minutes.

What are the top three things people do not like about receiving sales calls?

1 Lies ('This is a courtesy call . . . you have been specially picked . . . we specialize in people like you . . . you have won a holiday in Hawaii')

2 Script reading

3 Pushiness

What are the top three things people like when receiving sales calls?

1 Honesty and being straight to the point ('I am calling to persuade you to buy from me')

2 Listening and answering questions

3 Relevance

It is often amazing how quickly salespeople will drop their price. They clearly believe that this is the way to secure a deal. However, by discounting you are in danger of reducing your product's perceived value for money. Your profit is determined by your margin times the number of sales. If you halve the margin you will have to double sales.

What are you doing to raise the value of your product, relative to alternatives, in your customers' minds? Remember the golden rule: if in doubt, put prices up and sales will probably go up, not just in revenue but also in volume.

SKILLS AT TURNING IDEAS INTO PRODUCTS THAT SELL

Here is an exercise to train you in thinking about prospects from a marketing point of view.

1   You have invented a new machine that will cost about £5. It is a homing device to find anything you lose: mobile phone, keys, handbag, wallet, glasses.

2   Your task is to think of ten people to whom you can sell your invention.

Your thoughts might run like this:

1   People are constantly losing such items so you would immediately want to approach sellers of mobile phones, spectacles and handbags.

2   Insurance companies might have listings available of people that lose things (because they make claims).

3   Insurance brokers' offices might be a good prospect.

4   Some professions might have a specialized use for such a device.

5   The device could be used for easily locating people within a building.

6   People who do not know each other can identify one another at a
    meeting place.

7   You could sell it to your personal contacts so as to get some initial
    cash and feedback.

8   You can ask your network of contacts for their ideas.

9   You could talk to car retailers about buying in bulk and giving the
    device away to each customer as a promotion.

10 You could approach drivers' organizations to promote it.

Progress now

1. You have noticed whilst driving that the vast majority of cars carry no passengers. It occurs to you that you could set up an agency to organize lifts around the country. What you need is people travelling and people wanting lifts or things delivered to register with you.

2. The beauty of this idea is that you would not have to seek an investor to buy vehicles. Computers are so sophisticated now that you can buy a database that will link offers to wants. You will charge a 15 per cent arrangement fee to the vehicle owner. You will produce a mileage price list which all members must adhere to.

Having set up the systems, you now need to recruit drivers and customers to match together. Write down ten ideas as to how you can practically get the business off the ground.

_____

_____

_____

_____

_____

_____

SKILLS IN SPOTTING FUTURE TRENDS

Many entrepreneurs start by taking what they did for a big company and offering these services. Others start a business which is based on a hobby. These are good motivators, as they tend to bring passion, enthusiasm, knowledge and experience with them. However, they are missing one crucial element. Your focus to make money should be on what customers are going to buy in the future. Ask yourself this question and then ask how you can use your talents and experience to ride this wave. Find something that is on the increase. Put yourself five years into the future: what do you expect your industry to look like? Start by going back five years and write down ten things that have changed in that time. Where is society heading? What trends are gaining in force and are going to make major changes to how people spend their money? Make sure that your passion is matched by a set of customers.

A SKILL TAKEN FROM BRUCE LEE

In the opening sequence to one of his films, **Bruce Lee** taps a trainee on the head and says, 'Don't think . . . feel.' In martial arts, your focus needs to be both on your opponent and on any potential threat around you. Apply this philosophy and you will go far with marketing. You must be sensitive to how the customer will react and instinctively be there fast to meet their needs.

THE SKILL OF ILLUSION

When their companies are growing, entrepreneurs are often limited by working capital. A growing company always has a cash flow drag. One of the practical ways around this is to contract out some of the work until you are bigger. For example, you may have orders which you cannot satisfy because you cannot afford to employ enough staff. Why not subcontract the work to a competitor for a percentage off the top?

SKILL AT PERSISTENT MOTIVATION

In business, people need a lot of training and motivation to get over failure. Engineers seem to have a much better mindset. A mechanic fixing a car will gather information and make a judgement on what action has to be taken. If that does not work, they try something else until it does work. As they work they seem to find that the problem becomes more and more interesting. Scientists and engineers consider experimentation and getting lots of things wrong the natural path to success.

A significant skill is the ability to remain enthusiastic whilst enduring failure. Concentrate on the valuable lessons and opportunities each bad experience gives you.

Progress now

What skills do you need to concentrate on to develop as an entrepreneur?

_____

_____

_____

Chapter 9
The Happy Entrepreneur

If you suddenly lost all your material possessions, would you still be happy? I would.

SENSEI PAUL ELLIOTT

Whatever you are, be a good one.

ABRAHAM LINCOLN

WHAT MAKES A HAPPY ENTREPRENEUR?

Being a happy entrepreneur means making sure that all aspects of your life are satisfying as your success and wealth continue to grow. Some costs are not worth it: your health, your life partner and your family. Proceed wisely and these other aspects can be integrated to grow and flower with you.

When you pick any role model to learn their secrets, check first if they had or have happy lives. Many of the traits of successful entrepreneurs may come through negative experiences. For example, thrift is a common virtue which has often been created through an experience of hardship in childhood. This early experience can lead to feelings of insecurity which develop into an obsession to hoard money in order to feel safe. So they keep working hard, hoarding more and more money but never achieving true inner happiness.

So if you need a lot of money to feel secure a good therapist or personal coach could be a lot more effective than making a lot of money. Make happiness your overriding goal, for you and your family, and design a destiny for yourself that is truly fulfilling and deeply satisfying. That way all types of riches will flow towards you.

THOSE AT HOME

Keep your family informed of what is going on. Many entrepreneurs think that they have to protect their family from anything negative in the world. A good motive certainly. Yet your family also love you and need to feel they are supporting you during both the ups and the downs. In fact, if you share openly with them they can be a fount of support, ideas and encouragement.

Many entrepreneurs work all hours away from home, making lots of money and saying their motive is to give their children a better future. They do not even believe it themselves. You must make sure that, whatever your personal circumstances, when you look at your goals you consider your whole life and the other people in it.

FIT AND A FORTUNE

Being financially secure in your old age won't do you much good if your body does not last the distance. Entrepreneurs undoubtedly have to pay a price for their freedom to put their ideas into practice. That price should not include health or loved ones.

Stress can be burnt out of your system with exercise. In many other ways, your mind and imagination will work better if you are fit. To launch and build an enterprise you are going to have to work hard and be constantly motivated and full of energy, so you must maintain a high level of personal fitness and health.

A common pattern of dealing with stress is replacing a workout in the gym with a quick gin and tonic before dinner or a couple of cigarettes. This lifestyle leads to declining health, accelerated ageing and a whole range of health problems. No goal is worth this price.

The way to get healthy is to define doing exercise as part of your working hours. Budget for it in your timetable and consider it part of what you do to build your business. For all sorts of physiological reasons, the period after a workout is very productive for thinking. This is when many entrepreneurs get their best inspiration. For each hour invested in the gym, the return is an extra two hours of productivity the next day. The fact that you will live longer and more healthily is a good bonus.

Here are some tips that can change how you feel without any cost in terms of money or time:

- Replace all drinks with water for two weeks, and notice how much better you feel.

- Start each day with three slow and deep breaths.

- Go away for a long weekend each quarter. However, do something that decreases not increases stimulus to the senses.

- Build more walking into your habitual routines. Walking will improve your weight control, reduce stress, improve your mood and give you more energy.

MY BABY

Entrepreneurs tend to think of their businesses as their baby. If it is attacked, they react accordingly. Yet the idea in an enterprise never in fact comes to an end: it transforms into its next life cycle. Like a baby growing up, it learns from mistakes and keeps changing its form. Even liquidation is only a transformation if you allow it to be.

Companies fail, not entrepreneurs. Entrepreneurs evolve continually. The worst thing that can happen to you is bankruptcy, and this means that you no longer have any debts and can start something afresh with the added resources of all the knowledge gained. The reality of this scenario is much less frightening than the one people conjure up in their imaginations, fuelled by taking advice from people who do not know what they are talking about. If your personal and business relationships are built on trust and integrity, they will remain secure for the long term.

DON'T RISK YOUR RETIREMENT

Many entrepreneurs have not bothered with a pension for themselves, believing that their business is their pension scheme. Entrepreneurs certainly have the advantage, should they wish to, of not having to retire. But excellent entrepreneurs work from the assumption that if something can go wrong it will, and plan accordingly.

THE PATH WITH A HEART

During an entrepreneur's career there are many challenges that an employee does not face to the same degree. Your salary is not secure. What you have spent years building can come under threat. These pressures can test you, and the weak will succumb to the easy path. The right path requires strength of character and a high sense of honesty, integrity and responsibility to others. Real entrepreneurs are more about giving than taking. Being tuned into the needs of others gives them an advantage in seeing opportunities. If you are just looking for opportunities for your own gain, you will never realize true satisfaction and happiness.

MAKING THE WORLD A BETTER PLACE

When was the last time your thoughts were focused on what you could do for somebody else, without any benefit to yourself?

- ℚ If you found a £10 note on a shop floor, what would you do with it?
- ℚ If you see litter do you pick it up and put it in a dustbin?
- ℚ If you looked all day, could you not even find one cigarette end on the pavement?
- ℚ Would you feel safe late at night waiting for a bus alone in your capital city?
- ℚ If you lost your wallet in the street would you be totally confident that it would be returned via the authorities?
- ℚ Can you be 100 per cent confident that when you buy something that you will not be short changed?

There are many people in the world that can answer yes to all of those questions. A Tokyo newspaper once placed wallets full of cash all over the city streets . . . and all of them were handed in.

Entrepreneurs need to have a heart and a conscience, as they are able to make changes to society. It is important therefore to realize your responsibility for your actions. There is a world of difference between someone driven by a passion for something that they know will work and has a commercial opportunity and someone just going for profit.

The above questions also ascertain to some degree the quality of entrepreneur you are. Are you focused on others or yourself? Focusing on others makes better sales and marketing professionals. This focus enables them to have great empathy and connection with customers and thus make better decisions.

POSITIVE ENVIRONMENT: THE QUICK TICK TEST

Here is a practical test to see how much positive thinking and energy is around you.

Get a pen and pad of paper on a clipboard and mark three headings along the top: Positive, Indifferent and Negative.

Next time you are waiting for someone, put a tick against one of the three columns for each passer-by, judging them by their body language, expression, posture and speed of walking. Wait until 100 people have passed you and total up your three columns. Repeat the exercise in different locations, in different months or at different times of day to get more data. For example, you may notice a significant difference in people before and after Christmas.

People that look happy, excited or enthusiastic are very much in the minority. Remember that newcomers to a team will rapidly adopt the dominant mood of the group, whatever mood they begin with.

Negative people are allergic to positive energy and have many effective weapons in their arsenal to destroy positive energy thoughts, ideas and dreams. Avoid them at all times and surround yourself with positive people so that you are absorbing positive suggestions and influence.

Progress now

What unacceptable pressures are there on your life? What changes can you make now to bring them into alignment?

Chapter 10
Going For It

Empty pockets never held anyone back. Only empty heads and empty hearts can do that.

NORMAN VINCENT PEALE

If you don't take risks, it is very difficult to succeed.

VIJAY DHIR

FOCUS

In working out their goals, many entrepreneurs focus on houses, holidays and cars. It is more effective to focus on financial freedom as your goal. All the other things will come anyway. You are financially free when you have created enough wealth that your income from it, without depleting capital, is enough to live on. Having a lovely house with a larger mortgage, a car on loan and a holiday paid partly for by credit card is celebrating success before it has happened and does not lead to happiness. This is conditioning your mind to reward yourself without success, and this sets up bad habits that at best will hold you back and at worst will put you out of business.

So have houses, cars and holidays in your dreams but make sure that you reward yourself when you can really afford them by paying cash and remaining financially free. Once you are financially free you never want to risk losing this position. Focusing on being financially free is more supportive to running your business. It keeps your mind on cutting costs, making sales, creating new ideas, growing and investing.

215

THE SUCCESS DECISION

Entrepreneurship is a state of mind, an attitude and a decision. One of the secrets is taking control of your thoughts and making them work towards your goals.

To learn, you must challenge what you already know, do or believe in. Changing some of the routine things you do will teach you how to break patterns and make new choices.

Progress now

Write down three things that are great in your life right now.

1 _____

_____

2 _____

_____

3 _____

_____

MOTIVATION

🔊 If you were given the challenge of making £1 million in the next three months, could you do it?

🔊 If you had three months in which to make £1 million or you would lose all contact with your family and friends, could you do it?

Most people say no to the first and yes to the second. If this is you, what made you say yes?

Motivation is easy: it all depends on how much you want something.

CUSTOMER FOCUS

Many people in sales have needed their focus changing from their commission to the needs of the customer. Customers will tell you their needs freely and provide you with commercial opportunities. The best selling technique is to listen carefully and then offer something that truly addresses your customers' needs.

SALES CHANNELS

There is always more than one way to sell your merchandise. Here are some avenues for your consideration:

- Set up a group of sales agents
- Employ commissioned sales representatives
- Organize other companies to be resellers
- Give free talks, presentations or demonstrations
- Offer your products to a network marketing company or set one up yourself

FREE RESOURCES AROUND YOU

You are surrounded by great wealth, all available for you to use for free. Have you taken your share yet?

Progress now

Think of ten resources around you that can help to build your business.

1 _____

2 _____

3 _____

4 _____

5 _____

6 _____

7 _____

8 _____

9 _____

10 _____

WHAT STOPS YOU GOING FOR IT?

Barriers to entry in any particular industry vary but the most common ones are:

- Supporting a family and the mortgage
- Lack of finance
- Lack of suitable staff
- Lack of an established name

These are all excuses for not overcoming fear of some sort. Recognise this and work on your fears.

Fear is the biggest stopper: fear of losing your house, of poverty, of criticism or of failure. But if the pressure intensifies, it is best to get your head down and work. Your mind will be occupied with working – you will not have spare capacity for worry.

PRICING

Many customers will focus more on a discount than they do on the absolute price. They will also judge quality from the original price, not the discounted one. So if you want £25 for an item, ask for £35 and offer a special £10 discount.

When you are buying goods and services, only consider the asking price. Be wary of making judgements on what the price used to be. If there were buyers at this price, the supplier would not be offering a discount.

Progress now

Think of three failures or disappointments you have had in the past three months. Were there opportunities from each that you have missed until now?

1 _____

2 _____

3 _____

ONE THING AT A TIME

Be wary of having five great ideas and going for all of them. Focusing on one, making it work and then moving on to the next is a much more practical strategy for success.

If you are starting a new enterprise, your very newness can put off potential customers and suppliers. The latter look for cash payments until you have established yourself. To a potential customer, your being new means that your service may be more unpredictable than that of an established player. Making sure that the most important aspects of your business work smoothly will allay these fears.

NETWORKING

Make a list of all the people you could possibly contact to get your sales off the ground.

Progress now

1 Write a list of 100 people you know. How well you know them, or in what capacity, is irrelevant.

2 Write a second list of 100 people whom you have met through people on the first list. You now have your starting point to networking.

3 Go through the list and consider how each person could help you in your venture.

4 Ring them, tell them your plans and how they fit into them, and ask if they can help. Whatever their answer, ask them for two referrals and for any ideas.

KNOW WHAT YOU ARE UP AGAINST

Do your own survey of your competitors by ringing them with a sales enquiry.

- How many rings before they answered?
- How pleasant was the greeting (score out of 10)?
- Were you left hanging on?
- Do they ask for your name or number?
- Did they really want your business?

If you make sure that your people perform better than the above, you will rise above that competitor.

PRACTICALITIES OF RAISING MONEY

Most entrepreneurs apply their creativity to minimizing the financial resources they will need to get their venture under way. They will live on a survival budget, work all hours from home, convert the garage and buy secondhand. This way they can slowly build up sales with a minimum of overheads, learning as they go and getting the business model right.

Sometimes, though, raising significant finance can make what would happen in five years happen in one. Books on business will advise you that there are two main sources of finance: debt or equity. This means that you get a loan and pay interest or sell shares in return for a cash investment. In practice, both sources have benefits and disadvantages. For many entrepreneurs, the loan route will be limited unless they have considerable assets to secure the loan.

Do not be naive. If you walk into a bank with a fantastic plan for a business, you will probably be turned down. At some point the bank will ask you how much equity you have to secure the loan if your business fails. As their statistics will indicate, only one in a thousand businesses survives the first year. So expect to be rejected.

This is where the venture capitalists come in. In practice if you go this route your main cost can be the time you spend researching, developing, visiting, presenting and negotiating. You have to become an expert in something you will probably do only once.

The following sections describe the various ways in which many successful entrepreneurs have financed their businesses.

FACTORING / INVOICE DISCOUNTING

Factoring is a great idea for growth companies with continually increasing needs for working capital. The concept is simple. The finance company will give you what is effect a secured loan on your invoices out. In an entrepreneur company, the debtor balance is always growing and thus always causing more of a strain. Factoring will give you a percentage of your invoices on issue and charge you an overdraft-type interest rate. The finance company will also provide you with full credit control and legal services. If your business is paying out for contract labour on a weekly basis and being paid on 30- to 90-day terms, factoring can make the difference between being in or out of business. Bear in mind that, as you grow, your overdraft rate automatically goes up with your invoicing level.

Again, look closely at the small print of the agreement. Finance companies often want personal guarantees and initial deposits, both of which can often be negotiated out of the deal.

GRANTS AND AWARDS

Contact your local bank manager, Business Link, Training and Enterprise Council, MP, MEP, chamber of commerce, local networking group, trade or professional association and accountant. Big companies sometimes have a programme to support entrepreneurs. There are various grants available, particularly if you are set up in a relatively undeveloped area.

RETAINED CONTRACTS AND SUPPLIER FUNDING

Whatever business you are trying to launch, the retained contracts method is always worth consideration. Visit prospective customers and sign them up for a contract under which they pay one-third as an initial retainer for you to start work. (Never let them know just how dependent you are on the up-front payment.) **Aristotle Onassis** was a master of this technique. He started his shipping career by getting a contract for delivery then taking that to a bank in order to get a loan to buy a ship.

Another method in a similar vein is supplier funding whereby you produce to order and so avoid the need to manufacture and store stock. You may have to be very fast, so make sure you are prepared.

SUPPLIER CREDIT

When you have worked out your business plan, you will know what you need the money for. If you can negotiate 90-day terms with suppliers this could solve or considerably reduce your financial requirements. As you negotiate, make sure you keep their goodwill and offer them your longer-term business as you grow.

CONTINGENCY PAYMENTS

Instead of buying advertising space, negotiate a deal whereby the company can market your products for a cut. This way you have no advertising spend and a steady income stream without any incumbent fixed costs. Whatever your product or service there will be hundreds of websites interested in such a proposal. Pick sites that have the type of traffic that would be interested in what you offer.

WHO HAS AN INTEREST IN MY SUCCEEDING?

Ask yourself the above question. How can you use the answer to help your enterprise? Issuing shares to family and friends can be better than just asking for loans. This way they participate in the profits if all goes to plan and you do not have a debt if it does not. If you later need to raise further venture capital, it will look good to have more than just yourself as a shareholder.

CREDIT CARDS

Because credit card companies receive a percentage from the retailer and interest from you every time they are used, they are extremely lucrative for the issuer. The large amounts of fraud and defaults are tiny compared with the huge profits the credit card companies make, so they try to give out as many as possible.

Many major companies started by making use of multiple credit cards. Unlike the bank, they do not require you to spend a day a month preparing a report on how well you are doing. The interest rate will be high but you have given away no equity and it can get you off the ground with little fuss. Use them to get started then make paying them off as soon as possible a priority.

REVERSE FINANCING

Instead of bringing capital into your company, take the company to the capital. You can approach an existing larger company that is well funded and offer your enterprise together with you as a package. The larger company can have majority control and even a formula geared to performance to buy out your minority interest.

This way you can use the larger company's corporate resources and infrastructure without any extra spend and you will have an established name, contacts and market. Your venture will be far more secure and will have a greater chance of success. It is essential that the partnership is made with an organization that has synergy with your enterprise.

This is an ideal option if your objective is a capital gain and you are more interested in the value of your shareholding than the percentage. You could also use this route to sell out and have a significant cash resource for your next venture.

FRANCHISING

Be a franchisor. Franchising is a possibility when you have a business model that can be duplicated easily to autonomous units. Many small companies have grown through franchising without the need to raise large amounts of capital. The main danger is having franchisees who, being owners, want to call the tune all the time. You cannot control a franchisee in the same way as you can control an employed manager.

Progress now

With reference to your past five years and to what you want to achieve in the next five years, consider the following statement:

'What counts is not what talent you've got but how you use it.'

Chapter 11

Letting the Genie Out of the Lamp

> If we all did the things we are capable of doing, we would literally astound ourselves.
>
> THOMAS A. EDISON

> Most people give up just when they're about to achieve success.
>
> ROSS PEROT

GOING FORWARD

Corporate staff often have their natural entrepreneurial spirit lying dormant. For a corporation to encourage entrepreneurship – and many do – there must be no punishment in any form to anyone who makes a mistake or fails. If there is, personnel will seek to stay with the safe and secure.

Venture capitalists know that for every ten new ideas they invest in, nine of them will not make it. Yet the one that becomes a big success is worth all the others. It is the same with ideas. More often than not it is the failed ideas that lead to further work which creates something successful. Failure is the essential process that allows success. So if you have a corporate culture that punishes failure, you will not develop a breed of corporate entrepreneurs. It is this holding back of the entrepreneurial instinct that gives rise to so many new companies each year. At some point the entrepreneur inside an employee says 'enough is enough' and decide they to pursue their dream.

Often it is people from outside an industry that come up with successful ideas. So one of the problems you might face is that your strength area is the industry you are familiar with and you have bought into many of the established ways of doing things, which can hamper new perspectives. So, to be innovative the trick is to challenge all your assumptions and ask a whole series of 'why' questions.

It is clear that to be a good entrepreneur you must have a balance of different traits. For example, you must be both optimistic and pessimistic. Optimism is valuable in visualizing a potential market for your idea and to provide the daily drive to keep you going through thick and thin. Pessimism defends you against potential problems. Think ahead and try to predict everything that could go wrong. Then structure your business accordingly. A common defence is to ensure that the cost base is as low as possible. The lower it is, the longer you will withstand a cold wind.

MIND THE GAP

Predicting gaps that are emerging is where there is most opportunity.

A gap to an entrepreneur must be defined as something that is not being supplied or supplied well, which can or will satisfy a frustrated need. The same product at a better price through more efficiency of production might be the gap you are looking for. Don't forget, though, that if something is not currently available it could be because nobody wants it. So be mindful of any gap and examine any opportunity thoroughly in terms of costs and realistic sales and how those sales can be made.

INNOVATE TO PROSPER

People often think that entrepreneurs focus their ideas purely on creating new products or services. Ideas and innovation are equally important in running the business itself. If you have an idea to produce an existing product in a way that is far more efficient, you can compete for sales on price. In its early days, the **Ford** motor company turned its innovation and ideas not just to new and better cars but also to more cost-effective methods of production.

When companies do well and establish a lead, they gain advantages from economies of scale and greater brand awareness. It is often this comfort zone that stops them innovating, thus producing opportunities for entrepreneurs. Big companies can seem frightening competition, but as well as their advantages they also have several disadvantages.

Whatever dilemma you face, there are:

- ℞ Always three ways out of it
- ℞ Always three ways to turn it to your advantage
- ℞ Always three lessons to be learnt to improve your future decision making

NAME AWARENESS

When naming your enterprise, start by writing down a list of your objectives then match them to possible names. Using your own name might give your ego a great boost but will it encourage sales? Your name should be instantly memorable and should tell people what the enterprise does.

CASH COUNTS

Cash is your top priority, so always be aware of present and future movement of your cash. Entrepreneurs know that a sale is real only when the cash has cleared through the bank, whilst a purchase affects them only when they part with cash for it. If you keep it simple by planning to maximize the amount of cash in your bank, you will not go far wrong.

Progress now

Think of six companies that you have had dealings with in the past year: three that you had excellent customer service from and three where it was awful. Write your reasons.

Excellent customer service:

1 _____

2 _____

3 _____

Awful customer service:

1 _____

2 _____

3 _____

You now have a list of what to do and what not to do when you launch your own business.

THE ENTREPRENEUR LIFE OF JO FREEDOM

She wakes up early, raring to go. Passion for the day ahead fills her mind with energy. She owns an executive search firm that is one year old. She has worked hard to get clients on board. Jo spotted a niche in the market for qualified accountants with fluent second languages so she called her business Accountants Anywhere. She employs three staff, and although doing well, cash flow is a challenge and growth eludes her.

The first year was harder than she had expected. Previously, as a top performer in a leading firm, she never realized the advantages of an established name and a constant flow of candidates and clients. Her first month was spent looking for offices and her second designing and ordering stationery, from business cards to terms and conditions. Her third month was spent getting the web page up and running. Yet she was happy, the £25,000 overdraft facility was now just over £10,000 so the pressure was not on yet.

In month four she focused on recruiting staff, to get sales coming in. Her personal billings were virtually non-existent whilst she completed all these tasks.

By month five she realized that sales were less than she predicted in her budget and the costs more than double. There were many unexpected things coming up and no system to deal with them.

By month six, although sales were below target they were steadily rising nevertheless. Of course, the staff were paid commission long before payment was received.

By month seven her overdraft had reached £24,000, although she had reached breakeven. This meant that her invoices out and her placements not yet billed totalled £35,000. Debts to suppliers were just £2400. The office had demanded two months' rent in advance, so technically she had an asset sitting there. She had a 25 year lease, so at least her base was secure.

To build an executive recruitment business she had to look the part, so she arranged a £10,000 facility on her three credit cards and with them bought two top quality suits and a new car – nothing flash, but she had to travel a lot.

In month eight the bank telephoned, wanting to see her. She showed them her accounts and they agreed to maintain the overdraft at £25,000 for a further six months. Jo was expecting them to support her further but realized now that her house equity would not cover everything. It also came as a shock to her when the bank manager reminded her that they could call in the overdraft at any time.

What advice would you give Jo?

Progress now

What are the ten things that you would do from the start if you were Jo?

1 _____

2 _____

3 _____

4 _____

5 _____

6 _____

7 _____

8 _____

9 _____

10 _____

ANOTHER BITE OF THE CHERRY

If you are going off course, don't keep drifting. Your time as entrepreneur is your company's greatest asset. Staying until the ship goes down can take for ever and deny you the next opportunity. Stay focused on your long-term goal. This sometimes means abandoning the direction you are going in. Entrepreneurs continually reinvent their companies and ideas. The main asset of the business is you, so focus on that. If you are the asset, even liquidation cannot stop you from transferring your knowledge to your next venture.

If something fails, don't spend years drifting to a slow, inevitable end, hoping for a big break. Instead take all that you have learnt and make a better attempt next time. Each failure is a step to success. Read the biographies of famous entrepreneurs and you will realize that the secret of mirroring their success is to be found in studying not how they succeeded but how they reacted to their failures.

AS THE FUTURE UNFOLDS

Traditionally, small firms have taken on their bigger competitors by specializing. **Tie Rack** competed in one niche against major high street clothing retailers. But times change and it takes longer for big companies to adapt to those changes. Smaller companies can change much more quickly if they notice market trends.

Once you have got your business established and into profit you now have a choice: to stay small or to go for growth. It entirely depends on your motivations. Growth usually means increased risk. Taking a risk when you have nothing or little to lose is easier than when you have a significant asset to lose.

Many entrepreneurs go for growth, but more size can mean more problems. Expand only when you are bursting at the seams to supply orders that you already have. If you want to open a branch network, develop business in that area from your existing base and set up locally only after you already have a market there.

COMPLETE THE JOURNEY

Your drive will have to be very strong to keep you going. The advantage that entrepreneurs have is that they are doing exactly what they want to do, in their way and with full responsibility.

The same risk and fear that stops some people from even trying is the buzz that gets others to go for it. Those that have succeeded have these same fears but have used them as energizers and to fuel motivation.

Everyone has within them the creativity, drive and all that it takes to be a successful entrepreneur. It takes just three things: the motivation, an idea and some streetwise techniques.

spoils should his project eventually work. A barter system has started.

Over the years, the population grows and their needs change again. The economy is growing and prospering and a barter system has developed. However, this becomes difficult because the schoolteacher, for example, cannot offer much to those that do not have children. So a rudimentary currency is established by which everybody has to put a monetary value on their services. Market prices are settled by haggling and by the availability of alternatives.

Every time you feel a challenge, read this book – you will find it uplifting, inspiring and with many suggestions applicable to your needs.

Entrepreneur – go on, I dare you.

Biographies of Entrepreneurs

Alcraft, Rob, *Richard Branson* (Heinemann, 1998)

Bloomberg, Michael and Winkler, Matthew, *Bloomberg by Bloomberg* (John Wiley, 2001)

Bookbinder, Paul, *Simon Marks Retail Revolutionary* (Weidenfeld & Nicolson, 1993)

Brands, H.W., *Masters of Enterprise: Giants of American Business from John Jacob Astor and JP Morgan to Bill Gates and Oprah Winfrey* (Free Press, 1999)

Branson, Richard, *Losing My Virginity* (Virgin Books, 2000)

Chernow, Ron, *Titan: The Life of John D. Rockefeller Sr* (Warner Books, 1998)

Conran, Terence, *Q&A: A Sort of Autobiography (Habitat)* (Harper Collins, 2001)

Dyson, James, *Against the Odds* (Texere Publishing, 2000)

Forte, Charles, *The Autobiography of Charles Forte* (Sidgwick &

Jackson, 1986)

Frischauer, Willi, *Onassis (Aristotle Socrates Onassis)* (Bodley Head, 1968)

Higham, Charles, *Howard Hughes, The Secret Life* (Sidgwick & Jackson, 1993)

Horneshaw, Jane, *The Story of Henry Ford* (Collins, 1980)

Hurst, Margery, *Walking up Brook Street (Brook Street Bureau)* (Weidenfeld & Nicolson, 1988)

Kroc, Ray and Anderson, Robert, *Grinding It Out: The Making of McDonald's* (St Martins Press, 1990)

Lenzner, Robert, *Getty: The Richest Man in the World* (Hutchinson, 1985)

Lowe, Janet, *Bill Gates Speaks: Insight from the World's Greatest Entrepreneur* (John Wiley, 1998)

Mosley, Leonard, *Real Walt Disney: A biography* (Grafton, 1985)

Ortega, Bob, *In Sam We Trust: The Untold Story of Sam Walton and how Wal-Mart is Devouring the World* (Kogan Page, 1999)

Roddick, Anita, *Business as Unusual* (Thorsons, 2000)

Schulz, Howard, *Pour Your Heart Into It (Starbucks),* (Hyperion, 1998)

Shawcross, William, *Rupert Murdoch (News International)* (Pan, 1993)

Smith, Bob and Vlamis, Anthony, *Business the Yahoo! Way: Secrets of the World's Most Popular Internet Company* (Capstone, 2000)

Thomas, Bob, *Building a Company: Roy O. Disney and the Creation of an Entertainment Empire* (Hyperion, 1998)

Walton, Sam, *Sam Walton Made in America: My Story* (Bantam, 1993)

Wilson, Mike, *The Difference between God and Larry Ellison: Inside Oracle* (William Morrow, 2000)

Websites of entrepreneur interest

www.alexmcmillan.com
Author website with resources for entrepreneurs, including up to date links

www.startups.co.uk
Comprehensive online magazine for entrepreneurs

www.fsb.org.uk
Federation of Small Businesses.

www.dti.gov.uk
Department of Trade and Industry.

www.nban.co.uk
National Business Angel Network.

www.bvca.co.uk
British Venture Capital Association.

www.british-franchise.org.uk
The British Franchise Association.

www.franchise.org
The International Franchising Organisation.

www.sbs.gov.uk
Small Business Service of the government.

www.avondale-group.co.uk
Case study interviewee Kevin Uphill's enterprise offering advice on buying or selling a business.

www.eurodrive.com
Case study interviewee Richard Lowden's enterprise.

www.horshamkarateclub.co.uk
Case study interviewee Sensei Paul Elliott's enterprise.

www.cc-associates.co.uk
Case study interviewee Simon McBeth's enterprise.

Glossary

Business angel Wealthy individual looking to invest cash in companies with high growth potential in return for shares. Valuable experience, contacts and other support are often offered.

Business transfer agency Agency that sells businesses for a commission.

Corporate entrepreneur Ideas person within a company who introduces change.

Elevator pitch Summary presentation of a business proposal.

Equity Another term for shares in a company.

Factoring A system that raises immediate cash against sales invoiced as security.

Franchising A system that allows each operating unit to be owned and financed by a local entrepreneur in return for access to all the resources and support of the group.

Lifestyle business A business where profit maximization and growth are secondary to the owners doing what they love doing. By definition of limited interest to external investors.

Management buy-ins External management team buying a controlling shareholding and taking over the management of the company, usually with the backing of a financial institution.

Management buyouts Current management buying a controlling shareholding, usually with the backing of a financial institution.

NBAN (National Business Angels Network) Group of independent agencies around the UK that are introduction services between entrepreneurs and individual investors.

Network marketing A system that facilitates selling of goods and services by building up a network of distributors, that in turn recruits a network of distributors and so on. As the network grows so does the long-term passive profits of the distributor.

Opportunity directional questions Questions designed to help you come up with ideas.

Partnership A form of business trading which means that the individual partners and the business are one and the same thing from a legal standpoint.